Turning South Again

Turning South Again

Re-thinking Modernism/Re-reading Booker T.

Houston A. Baker Jr.

DUKE UNIVERSITY PRESS *Durham & London* 2001

Printed in the United States of
America on acid-free paper ♾
Designed by Amy Ruth Buchanan
Typeset in Carter and Cone Galliard by
Tseng Information Systems, Inc.
Library of Congress Cataloging-in-
Publication Data appear on the last
printed page of this book.

As I grow older, my southern accent thickens.

. . . .

Accepting its sweetness and bitter illusions
I've lived four-fifths of my life in this South
that believed in a lie we all still suffer for.
This long-owned land owned men.

JAMES APPLEWHITE, "Escaping Gravity"

Contents

Prologue

Blue Men, Black Writing, and Southern Revisions

A seed-time of quick violence
And hours resonant with despair,
Growing in this southern town
Was against the law,
Each green shoot lopped off. . . .

There was no sunshine six days a week;
On Sunday it beamed for ecstatic religion, and
Settled at dusk to a blood-red and sinful sky.

Finding my way through texts on family shelves,
I talked of Candide *and Copernicus*
To the stunned horror of others,
Became prey to charges of literacy
As hooked knives of the South swung low
To carry me home:
Black sufferers demanded my head
(on a platter)
And white women hinted worse.

Through this spawning time I read on, praying
For a moment to confide its truth,
In later hours ringing with despair,
To engage the burden of literacy (thank God!)
In the open air.

"City of My Youth," HOUSTON A. BAKER JR., *Blues Journeys Home*

What follows represents a black southern mind navigating oceans and landfalls of memory, ineradicable dilemmas of *black modernism,* protocols of black male subject formation. The primary "text" commences with specific blue/black memory . . . my own . . . gazing today out clear glass in North Carolina dawn, gazing north and west to my first recall of the first blackness of blue men I have encountered.

The very first Blue Man I remember was not Elmore James or Big Bill Broonzy but a vividly reported monster who was said to live somewhere in the vicinity of Louisville's Chicasaw Park—perhaps a dank cave clawed out of steep embankments dropping to the Ohio River. The Blue Man was grotesque, of uncertain origin, and his story was chilling. He was stealthy, yet ferocious, fanged and vicious in pursuit of young black men. This much was certain: boys who related the latest Blue Man sightings to my wide-eyed, trembling cohort claimed he was a relentless stalker of elementary school black boys like me. Yet he was no sensational or headlined serial killer. When on the verge of tears and hysteria I refused to climb forbidding third-floor stairs to my bedrooom, my father snapped open the *Louisville Courier-Journal* and showed me page by page by page. "You see," he said, "there isn't anything in here about a Blue Man. They are just trying to scare you, son."

My parents were middle-class, college-educated, and said they didn't believe in ghosts.

My brother and I were not allowed to read horror comic books; only Captain Marvel was acceptable among superheroes. To this day I don't know whether it was Superman's cowardly masquerade as a mild-mannered journalist, or his less-than-admirable susceptibility to kryptonite that landed him on our father's comic book index. But even if there was no room for everyday monsters in our household, the Blue Man would not be "disappeared" by parental fiat. He endured, tumesced, became ever more horrific in the storied assaults he launched on black flesh. Virginia Avenue Elementary School, in all the decorum of its proper and racially segregated protocols of Negro behavior, was no match for the Blue Man. For, as I now realize, the Blue Man was a pure product of black southern boyhood rumor, a sinister function in a continuous narrative that was always enhancing itself. The narrative was a grab bag containing snatches of colorful adult conversation, grim details of an Illinois black teenager mutilated and killed in Money, Mississippi, flashes from the Negro newspaper (the *Louisville Defender*) about police beatings and tavern brawls in black communities. There was enough tense, vaguely understood fear and anxiety in the air we breathed and enveloping territories we negotiated to provide tons and tons of narrative stuff to enlarge the Blue Man's existence.

Of course, I had no such geographically specific or narratologically reasoned defenses against terror when I was a boy in the South. I was scared out of my mind at my father's command to head up those dreaded third-floor stairs. I suspect that at such moments I was pretty closely akin to Percy Bysshe Shelley, who bolted screaming from the house in the middle of his wife Mary's recounting of her recently written tale, *Frankenstein*. But for me, there was no out. All my compeers were party to terror, rumor, reaffirmed savageries of the Blue Man. There was nothing for it but to climb the stairs, hoping what dreams ensued were less nightmarish than the previous night's fare, or the day's most recent tales of the Blue Man.

Wonder of all! Just as he emerged full-storied and terrible, the Blue Man vanished. He dropped from day-to-day oral tradition, replaced, of course, by other rumored stalkers of young black male flesh. Somehow though, these replacements seemed more manageable. We were older. We were growing up. The 1957 souped-up-Ford-car-driving bully "Big Ant" became more feared and legendary among us than rumors of night manglers emanating from misty caves in the segregated public park. And yet the object world of real villains was always, for me, tinged with hints of blue. Who was that murderous creature who walked my dream corridors like an escapee from Hieronymus Bosch? Why did he ally with a sense of sin, unworthiness, threat, guilt, terror? Somehow it still all seems quite removed from any run-of-the-mill economies of the ghost story . . . a rather different and far more terrifying haunting that seems related specifically to southern black life.

If my southern calculus of immediate fear entailed serious revision by the time I and my cohort reached a segregated Madison Junior High School, it was not because the aura of the Blue Man had departed our lives. We had simply stopped talking about him, concentrated our attention on deuce-and-a-quarter Ford engines, and turned much of our best attention to pretending the South was not all that bad for black adolescents . . . if you were going steady and had a television in your household.

We thus commenced those improvisatory rituals of black southern manhood revision. From the feverish ghoulish narrative collective unconscious of the Blue Man, we launched ourselves like leaping-hormone astronauts of "soul" into postures of *strategic forgetting and tensional rewriting*. We began publicly and energetically orchestrating Black Bad Man boasts of our imagined futures.

But . . . when after a party at the segregated YMCA, wind chilling our bodies moist still from the sensuous last slow dance, a corner of orange vodka left in the finger-printed pint bottles as we sped down Broadway Street . . . when the red lights of the Louisville police cruiser suddenly swooshed into the Ford's rear window, we knew we had gone nowhere.

The Blue Man never lived anywhere but in our minds. Like the men in blue who have immemorially been "pulling us over" because we are black, the Blue Man was always, already, everywhere in our everyday black male southern lives.

Decades later and late in our education, some of us Louisville boys have been blessed by literacy. We have a different take on that primal Blue Man. We know there are forms and performances we can articulate to substantiate and place him in the liberating economies of black mobility. Such articulation is less the work of dreams, badman boasts, material accumulations (though these are not without efficacy) than of writing.

Writing demands, or is perhaps the serendipitous offspring of, maturation, modicums of insight, measures of articulate memory.

What I shall call memorial and performative writing is our rite of black revisionary survival par excellence. In the most profound ways, writing, and especially revisionary writing, is our key to sanity, our prophylaxis against civil and social death.

By now it is pure cliché in the poststructuralist academy that the "self" is ever inside and inescapably constituted as writing, the symbolic order, the prison house of language. Ah yes, but for me and my black southern cohort concerned with black male subject formation, *writing* was specifically a performative act, endlessly attempting to master unique variations of Big Ant's "gangster lean" as he gunned his gleaming black and tan '57 Ford, preparatory to blowing away yet another soi-disant Bad Nigger from somewhere other than the "Big L" (Louisville).

Writing was our black defense against and revision of ancient terrors, mistaken identities, dread losses. We paragraphed ourselves with bravado into Jim-Dandy-to-the-Rescue dapperness of spirit to carry us through white Louisville's mean downtown streets unimpeded by youthful visions of snaggle-tooth, slow-drawling Blue Men biting off our heads. Those of us lucky enough to arrive at adolescent writing even got blessed and anointed by Dr. Martin Luther King Jr. and legions of local black elders' oratory—a civil disobedience linguistics that integrated schools, theaters, swimming pools, restaurants, department store dressing rooms. Dr. King and the elders issued a serious Blue Man abeyance order . . . a cease-and-desist, prior restraint on black physical and mental derogation of the spirit in our hometown.

But this is not a chronicle. It is a prologue. So, let me on the basis of the foregoing revery venture a hypothesis. (Too grand a word maybe. Those of my Louisville cohort who are still alive might consider what I am proposing simply a banal morsel of common sense.) Hypothesis: Louisville's horrific Blue Man and his ever creatively multiplying variations in our black male imaginary—paralyzing dreams, night terrors, darkly circulating rumor—were our elementary, and initiatory, black southern writing/performance. Storied, theoretical at base, and memorial, the Blue Man was metonym for the rigors of southern black male subject formation. I now, revisionarily, proclaim from middle age that such imaginative recitals as the Blue Man were our mythicohistorical archive of black incarceration in the Americas, a monitory chest of bones drifting from fathomless Atlantic depths, a figurative emblem for levitations of mutilated black bodies from burial grounds in piney woods turpentine camps, weeping corpses of cut-down virile black bodies felled by Trusty Shooters at Parchman Farm. Our Blue Man was racial memory mythically codified for childhood warning, self-definition, and defense. Blue Man was the oral-cultural and symbolically narrated realization of our black male place in confining spaces, framed by shape-shifting and ever threatening apparatuses designed to harm the black body. Remember: the Blue Man was denizen of the "colored" Chicasaw Park. He stalked exclusively young black males like me. He was an imaginatively activated, haunting recording and rehearsal of omnipresent southern dangers to mind, body, and soul of the black male subject. In time, headlined whites like Orville Faubus and James "Bull" Connor were adequate objective correlatives of southern blue and blues threat and disaster. But in our 1950s and earliest 1960s years of black upbringing, our language/exchange/performance was what might be called a strategically collective and theoretically primitive ritual of self-defense named the Blue Man. Language was our peer group's improvisational fluidity of revision and defense, our sometimes hortatory, always colorfully sublimating, projectional interlocution. *Writing* was our global explanation and prediction of what could happen to our black bodies under conditions of southern maleness. It was our *theory.* Writing was our racial group entrée into recesses of calculated confinements, carceral spaces whose import we could verbally approach only in the manner of cautious aviators over a battle zone. We were fliers who had yet to read the full text of the war. Little did we realize that our linguistics of the Blue Man were the ontogeny of southern black male subject formation. Yet it *was* our anticipatory self-defense. If needed, we could summon an articulate revisionary grace against the assaults of men in all-American blue, who would, on some indeterminate future sunny day, arrest, insult, pin us down on the all-purpose white man's charge: "You are hereby charged for blackness . . . the nigger in you!" We wrote. We performed. We created a manifold dramatis personae. We generated endless linguistic plotlines as archival, revisable resources against the implicit reality and actual day of our arrest. We read each others' body aesthetics, studied the hip limp of ghetto hustlers, practiced lines and stage blocking at home and in the streets with choral sounds of urgency, a vernacular doo-wop aimed at violence like that captured by the black prison poet Etheridge Knight.

> Well, shit, lil sis, here we are:
> You and I and this poem.
> And what should I do? should I squat
> In the dust and make strange markings on the ground?
> Run sister run . . . the Bugga man comes!

Knight's lines are from a poem titled "The Violent Space."[1] The Blue Man, the men in blue, our blues chants of black male subject formation converged in a violent space, haunted by a brutal past rife with underground/underocean black corpses of history. We wrote, we ran, we improvised, and some of us were blessed with life and the opportunity to continue writing toward black modernism. We have flowed ever toward endless revisions of blueness. And the new millennial present brings figurative and theoretical imperatives to our quest for the black modern undreamed in the philosophies of my black southern youth. Which of us, for instance, could have conjured the abyssal horrors of America's twenty-first-century *private* prison-industrial complex?

"Figuration" is the omnibus sign for black male subject formation's *défense légitime*. We know and we know, what forestalls our *modern* is not black male failure at a formal regimen of daily virtues à la Benjamin Franklin, or some genetically coded educational shortcoming, economic deficiencies, or pathological fears of liberty's incumbencies. What forestalls, forecloses, makes our quest for the *modern* ever renewing and Sisyphean is, in fact, the eye and body of the

Law—as the scholar Alan Hyde details these matters in his fine book, *Bodies of Law*. Let us look, for a figurative moment, at the notorious 1864 case before the Virginia supreme court, *Hudgins v. Wright:*

> *Three women about to be sold out of state as slaves sue on grounds they are of Indian ancestry. Witnesses are called, appearances scrutinized, there appear to be no (in the phrasing of Justice St. George Tucker) "flat noses" or "wolly hair." The women are determined free.*

Hyde writes:

> *Hudgins v. Wright* marks the moment when the legal concept of race changed from genotype to include also phenotype (appearance); when race ceased to be simply a kind of shorthand for genetic background and became rather a kind of embodied spectacle. . . . Race in American law is . . . unthinkable without a body and an eye. The body displays race, but only as perceived by the eye of the chancellor.[2]

In our black southern male subject formation, we could run, riff, and revise—performing against the grain and gore of archived American horror—but we could rarely simply outrun the blue, obscene gaze of the southern white chancellor's "eye-and-I." For that eye was the all-seeing judge of our sentenced confinements. So . . . like Robert Hayden's ship's recorder in the brilliant poem "Middle Passage," on many an evening those of us who had become prey to literacy wrote on paper or in imagination "[we] cannot sleep, for [we] are sick with fear, but writing eases fear a little since still [our] eyes can see the words take shape upon the page and so [we] write, as one would turn to exorcism."[3] Hayden's recorder is the chancellor, in despair at blackness. We, black males in formation, wrote blues.

Leaving off theoretical digression, let me return to my enrollment at twelve years of age at Louisville's Madison Junior High School. It was a rough transition—changing classes, complete incompetence with combination locks, muscled-up working-class boys irked to violence (against me!) by my "standard English" grammar of speaking. I must have looked like the dickens one evening because my dad took a rare time out from his evening self-improvement writing and said: "Hous, you know what scared the absolute hell out of me when I was about your age?" "No," I mumbled through tears that were annoyingly beginning to form. "Well," he said, "it was the Blue Man. He scared me to death." Dad had my full, incredulous attention. "But you and Mom said there was no Blue Man, Dad. You even showed me the newspaper." He smiled, half-amused, and said, "Yes, Hous. But you're older now."

His words were my adolescent, memorial, revisionary introduction, of course, to the parental world of black male subject formation in the United States South. Now, older still, and in the following pages, I write revisionarily, as "one would turn to exorcism." Eternal returns and full circles, negotiating postmodern roadblocks, feared assaults on body and consciousness, high-tech handcuffs and tracking systems in the blue of our country's prison-industrial complex. I often stay awake at night. Ghostly emanations of southern economies of violence against the black body toss and turn me. I have nightmares populated by posh-suited apologists for millions of African bodies displaced and disappeared by a Euro-American consumer revolution and transatlantic trade. The "suits" say it was all a *past* mistake. We should forget about slavery and "transcend" (whatever that implies) *race.* Meanwhile, Texas, Louisiana, Oklahoma "chancellors" signal the executioners of black and brown men and women on death row to get on with their blue work. All these haunting nocturnal horrors make running revision of the *black modern* an inescapable writing for my black turn-of-the-millennium southern scholarship. And, indeed, a new southern studies is long past due. I believe it must proceed, at least in part, by way of writing, running, revisionary accounts and naming of the present and present-day facts of United States crimes against the black American spirit; the stamps and mutilations "paid" of black male bodies swinging in southern winds, or dragged to decapitation on a Texas highway; the real-world starvation of a quarter of the children in a United States of America that brags of a "strong economy"; the forty-plus rounds of Blue Man ammunition fired, nineteen slugs entering the body of Amadou Diallo; the murderous shot of guards in summer 1999, bringing down the body of a young black man fleeing across a North Carolina prison farm field . . . running. I write now with such actually existing United States racial horrors as these staring me in the face. I write as a black male scholar positioned at a southern site of enunciation where there are major rewards for sycophancy, for solacing talk of "race transcendence" by putatively new black "Public Intellectuals." But mostly (and thankfully) I live and write now as a black male southerner who happily and compulsively cannot stop writing . . . or being black . . . or shrug off or sever the fibrous southern tenacity of my youth.

What follows, therefore, is not a rollicking, jestful fireside recollection of "Colored people." There is no happy account of bawdy Negro culinary predilections (fried chicken and other such stuff) south of Mason-Dixon. What follows is a revision of my scholarly self and opinions that is, at least in part, a function of my shudder at the utter terribleness of our new millennium.

However, there is more at stake in the following pages than "reactionism" or a merely performative revisionism. Perhaps the crux of what follows is preeminently an outgrowth of what I hypothesize as the always incumbent revisitation linked to black male subject formation. Such formation, I believe, dictates combing archives, annals, mythicohistorical lines of a black southern past that is, in very profound and undeniable ways, *the* past of *the* Americas. I hope to make all of this persuasively clear in my central text.

Malcolm X averred that "Mississippi" was anywhere in the United States south of the Canadian border. Searching revisionarily the geography, economics, race relations, demographics of the United States at our turn-of-the-millennium moment is vital work, not only for an energetic new southern studies, but also for a new—and expansive—American cultural studies. The further and, for me, most encouraging prospect of such running revision is the possibility that we might articulate and comprehend new scholarly, activist possibilities for projecting a *liberating black modernism*. I have in mind, by such a phrase, an achieved modernism, facilitating a black public sphere assembly and exchange capable of producing focused speaking and life-enhancing change for the black majority. Setting the Americas on a more even southern keel is a premiere scholarly task of the present.

As back beat for the revisionary account that follows—an account that commences with my worrying the line of two haunting scenes from the Afro-American literary canon—I wish I could provide a repertoire of percussion and rhythmic incantational Parchman Farm Prison song. Such song, like our narrative changes in the Louisville of my youth, suggests both the improvisatory character of any southern-sounded liberation of black spirit—what might be termed, that is to say, the shrewdly ineluctable mobility of black voice.

However, such a back beat as Parchman song (properly rendered) gives us would also remind us of the wisdom of the Parchman song caller "Bama," who told his interrogator, "If you bring a brand-new man in here [to Parchman Farm], if he had a voice where he could sing just like Peter could preach, and he didn't know what to sing about, well, he wouldn't be no good."[4]

In the office of the black modern, we inescapably sing about lockdowns, terrors of Blue Men, the living summons to witness our dead. I conclude then not with a song, but a poem . . . and hope the poem's implicit mandate is, in many ways, fulfilled by revisionary pages of the central text that follows. Roger Jaco, in 1979, writes from Rustburg (Virginia) Correctional Unit 9 as follows:

Easter
With captured friends
beneath the dull coolness
of a concrete sky
I sit and sweat
inwardly.
Drenched in bitterness
smelling of remorse,
we tug and strain
under laden backpacks

of unwanted time.
God, if only,
damn it if only
we could give it to the dead
we could all be
resurrected.[5]

Modernism's Performative Masquerade: Mr. Washington, Tuskegee, and Black-South Mobility

It seems to me there is rarely such a combination of mental and physical delight in any effort as that which comes to a public speaker when he feels that he has a great audience completely within his control.

BOOKER T. WASHINGTON, *Up from Slavery*

This capacity to switch enacted roles when obliged to do so could have been predicted; everyone apparently can do it. For in learning to perform our parts in real life we guide our own productions by not too consciously maintaining an incipient familiarity with the routine of those to whom we will address ourselves. And when we come to be able properly to manage a real routine we are able to do this in part because of "anticipatory socialization," having already been schooled in the reality that is just coming to be real for us.

ERVING GOFFMAN, *The Representation of Self in Everyday Life*

sweep . . . *to carry or trail along in a stately manner, as a flowing garment . . . to row, or to propel (a vessel), with sweeps or large oars . . . to pass a broom or brush over the surface of (something) so as to clear it of any small loose or adhering particles*

OXFORD ENGLISH DICTIONARY

I

The discussion that follows had its origin in what can only be called re-vision. First, there was the recall of my own youth in Louisville, Kentucky—a turning back to earlier days that is part and parcel of a memoir I am presently writing. Second, there was the haunting recurrence of two scenes from Afro-American literature that would not leave me alone. Since I have written about both scenes earlier in my career, their refusal to stay at rest combined with memoir to create a captivating regress: past personal life, past literary scenes, past literary criticism. One of the literary scenes that kept recurring is found in Ralph Ellison's novel *Invisible Man*.[1] It involves the unforgettable character Jim Trueblood. Describing his dilemma when faced with the incestuous abuse of his daughter, Trueblood says that he was in a "tight spot," and his task was to "move without moving" (46). The second scene is found in the exposition of Booker T. Washington's *Up from Slavery*.[2] Washington reports his anxieties upon receiving an invitation to deliver one of the opening addresses to the Atlanta Cotton States and International Exposition in September of 1895:

> I knew . . . this was the first time in the entire history of the Negro that a member of my race had been asked to speak from the same platform with white Southern men and women on any important National occasion. I was asked now to speak to an audience composed of the wealth and culture of the white South, the representatives of my former masters. I knew, too, that while the greater part of my audience would be composed of Southern people, yet there would be present a large number of Northern whites, as well as a great many men and women of my own race. (130)

On the morning he travels to deliver his speech, Washington says he "felt a good deal as I suppose a man feels when he is on his way to the gallows" (131). While journeying, he encounters a Tuskegee white farmer who says: "Washington, you have spoken before the Northern white people, the Negroes in the South; but in Atlanta, tomorrow, you will have before you the Northern whites, the Southern whites, and the Negroes all together. I am afraid that you have got into a tight place" (142).

"Tight places" are constituted by the necessity to articulate from a position that combines specters of abjection (slavery), multiple subjects and signifiers (Trueblood's narrative is produced for a rich, northern, white philanthropist), representational obligations of race in America (to speak "Negro"), and patent sex and gender implications (the role of the Law as the Phallus).

Though I had written about both Ellison and Washington, my memoiristic encounters with my own Louisville, Kentucky, youth obviously triggered something peculiarly southern as I sought a language of recovery for my past. Certainly, I have worked to make the language of my memoir more than a simple lyrical metaphysics of memory intended "for colored only." And surely I want my language of memory to transcend chest-thumping "end-of-racism" triumphalism intended for white readers alone. Somehow my own desires in the language for memory kept calling up those two scenes from Washington and Ellison.

After sleepless nights, I concluded that the alliance among the literary scenes mentioned and my memoir was geographical, gendered, and psychologically overdetermined. In a word, all involved the South, black men, and a certain species of performance anxiety. Furthermore, all were implicated to one extent or another with modernism, with finding a black voice that if it did not *transcend* the past would at least ameliorate, accommodate, and critique the past in ways confidently articulate with what the majority of black people require (especially *racially*) for the present and future.

My present work, therefore, involves re-vision and revisitation (much in the manner of the father's ghost in *Hamlet* that will not allow the prince to rest), and it begins for me with the inescapable fact of a tightly spaced "southernness" I have long sought to erase from my speech, my bearing, and my memory. But it has never really been possible. For in face-to-face encounters anywhere below the Mason-Dixon, I quickly discover I have not left the South, nor has the South left me. The vowels of my "educated black man" speech desert me almost instantly, and the slow-motion roll and drawl of

Kentucky syllables drip softly from my tongue. On such southern occasions, I feel ironic pride that I can still pull off the correct local pronunciation of my hometown "Louisville," which in the native, non-Francophone roll of things is "Lew-vull." In "Lew-vull," I first encountered the South . . . although our town's ambivalent boast was always that we were a regional borderland: the "Gateway to the South." Yet we were never reluctant to break into Stephen Foster melodiousness or to throw a respectful salute to gray-haired colonels, especially during Kentucky Derby season at Churchill Downs. "Gateway" meant, of course, very different things to very differently situated people.

For my older brother and me, it meant we could get out of "the South" and greet freedom simply by crossing the Ohio River. When our father acted on one or another of his peculiar lightings out for the Territory, he would command our mom to pack a picnic lunch, round up the boys, and get ready because we were going to Cincinnati and the zoo, or to an integrated theater where we could experience 3-D movies at first hand, or even stay overnight in a real hotel that would not turn us away at the desk because they did not serve "colored people." Midway the bridge over the river was a sign that read "Welcome to Ohio!" My brother and I would begin to shout and wrestle about in the back seat: "We're free! We're free! We're free!" Of course, on the return trip was a sign that read "Welcome to Kentucky!" And no matter what kind of time we had enjoyed across the river, we knew we were not gateway tricksters, but black southerners after all. As W. E. B. Du Bois might have stated it: "It is a peculiar burden, this incumbency of a black man's calling the South home." Countee Cullen, too, might have spoken of the irony of making a black man southern and bidding him to sing.

For at my "home" in Lew-vull, black people were shaped in exclusion, beguiled by white illusion, and deemed seriously delusional if they believed the Old South and its ways would ever give birth to brightness. So, today, when I find myself in Richmond, Raleigh, Greenville, New Orleans, Tuscaloosa, or Tugaloo, it only takes the half-hour ride from the airport with my host to set me back fifty years to the certainty, syllables, and immobilizing terror that often informed my Old Kentucky Home. Oh, it is true that sometimes I don't require a human voice at all. The particular song of a southern summer bird will do it, or if I am driving, it can be rounding the bend of a two-lane road and seeing black men butchering a hog suspended from a tree in the front yard of their cinder-block house. The special smell of jasmine and early-evening humidity powers up southern memory for me as megadoses of creatine do an athlete's muscles.

My head contains furious recall of Cassius Marcellus Clay as a rank amateur boxer (skinny, light-skinned boy who thought he was "pretty") knocking out opponents on the screen of our family's first, seventeen-inch, black-and-white television set on Saturday afternoons. The autobiographical bass rumblings of beer-drinking men on the porch of our store who boasted about how they had bested (or "whupped") some foul "cracker" or another. The aching beauty of the whole tabooed enrollment of young white girls sashaying the corridors of Western Junior High School on the first day of public school integration in Louisville. (O brave new world that hath such people in't! And in straight skirts no less.) My black peers' rhymed/signifying warnings against such beauty and desire: "Lord will I ever? Will I ever?!" And the Lord's reply: "No, Negro. You will never. *You* will never!" My parents were sort of like the Lord, I guess. Because they didn't think integration matters were all that wondrous either. At least not if integration was going to cause me and a goodly number of my peers to go to Western Junior High School, which was located in the Portland section of town. Portland was river-front, white working-class territory, and my parents considered it more *déclassé* than dangerous. My father asserted without seeming thought: "Son, those white crackers are poor, and I don't believe they are very smart, and I know they do not like colored folks. Why do you want to be with them?"

The catalogues of memory are endless, of course. What surprises me nowadays is that there seem so many triggers that set me talking about my southern home, even to bored or indulgent strangers on airplanes. Somewhere, somehow it must all have left an indelible and shaping ambivalence because, often despite myself, I display a badge of honor in regard to tight places of youth, tight places that were my testing ground, that are my legacy. Oh, it is not even remotely akin, I believe, to Quintin Compson's majestic and justifiably famous repetition compulsion: "I don't hate the South! I don't hate the South!"[3] For as surely as I am memorially in the South and it is in me, just as surely do I hate the South. Perhaps though, this is simply because "home" always has for us . . . as species . . . an opponent composition of aversion-and-attraction, which can take form as a compulsive, microscopic, and deeply ambivalent rehashing of the past. Where the South and black southern being are concerned, I believe such rehashing forms the crux of a psychodrama of framing, performance, signification, and, ultimately *being* for the black American.

II

One might say that *being framed* for the black American is being indexed by—and sometimes *in*—the South. This is so primarily because at the moment of joy marked by the Emancipation Proclamation, more than four million of the United States's five-million-plus black Americans were enslaved residents of the American South. And as the nineteenth century came to a close, over 90 percent of black Americans still resided in the South. The "frame," then, not only for an ambivalent southerner like me but also for an entire culture, might be seen as what the still infinitely readable W. J. Cash called "the mind of the South."[4] Mental attitudes and habits of mind, soul rhythms, ethical assessments, intellectual judgments, somatic adaptations, nocturnal anxieties, academic ideologies of black being in America are most profoundly imbricated with "the mind"—and here one must surely add the very bodies and demographics—of the South.

Cash's 1941 classic titled *The Mind of the South* is one of those books of meticulous research, regional critique, and felicitous prose that seem rare products of an academic era long past. What is most compelling about his work is that its thesis is so firmly supported by discussions of so many varying aspects of the southern mind.

Politics, religion, rhetoric, manners, education, morals, and, preeminently, economics and labor are among the broad range of his topics.

What Cash proposes is that any neat distinction between an "Old South" and a "New South" is made at one's peril. For the *mind* that drives the body in each of the areas of endeavor analyzed by Cash was formed, he contends, in the earliest, first-frontier days of the region below the Mason-Dixon. Excluding Virginia gentility from this first formation, Cash sees the South as a place of romanticism, resistance to intellectual analysis, resolute action as the mark of frontier individualism, earnest mythification of the "planter class" as akin to nobility, and a proto-Dorian code of class-coalition that allowed even back-country farmers to feel allied in their "whiteness" with wealthy planters, and vice versa. All of these formative regional characteristics were held in place, embellished, even defended in a disastrous and apocalyptic Civil War, by the economics of black slavery. Black slavery's formulation in a specific body of *slave law*—from the seventeenth century onward through its functional, if not nominal, manifestations in southern agriculture, industry, commerce, and labor well into the twentieth century—is critical. Of the post–Civil War world of the South, for example, Cash writes:

> as soon as [President] Andrew Johnson began to hand [white southern landowners] back the governments of their various states, they everywhere set themselves, before everything else, to the enactment of the famous vagrancy and contract laws—everywhere, that is, struck with characteristic directness in action, straight to the heart of their problem and sought at a stroke to set their old world whole again by restoring slavery in all but the name. (107)

The South defined itself in *difference* through the "peculiar institution" of black slavery.

Slavery made possible the southern mind's emergence, as it were, out of the cultivation and radical dependence upon two cash crops—cotton and tobacco. These two crops were brutally forced upon hundreds of thousands of acres of land they devastated, upon millions of black bodies subjugated to the status of slave, tenant farmer, sharecropper, black convict lease laborer, prisoner from Parchman Farm, chain gang laborer. The difference in the condition of the black body as cultivator before and after the Civil War was, according to Cash, that things got *much worse* for blacks *after* the war. For after the war, there was less food, fewer provisions for clothing, scanty "shelter" only in green-pine clapboard shanties.

What southern life consisted in after the war was, most abundantly, cheap labor. Remember, millions of black men, women, and children after the war became part of a competitive and supposedly "free" labor market. Black freedmen were supposed to be free to compete for forty acres and a mule wherever they chose. Of course, such economic freedom nowhere became a reality. And, in fact, it is Cash's contention that the South only adopted doctrines of "Progress" and "Prosperity"—with their symbols in the factory and paeans to commerce and industry—as a way of avoiding race warfare, between "free" black and white labor. The institutionalization of the cotton mill and textile factory provided a way to siphon off a "white labor surplus." Whites migrated from the fields and took up residence and work in mill towns and factories. A black enslaved agriculture, however, remained in place after the war. For, the very founding principle of southern mills, factories, and cotton-mill "villages" was "for whites only." Ironically, a rudimentary and technical schooling for blacks began to find white southern advocates at the same time segregated cotton-mill factories emerged. Of what use, though, would technical training be in the South for a technically educated black young man or woman who was forbidden access to technical "factory" work? The southern cotton mill and its village were scarcely, then, markers of *modernity,* or of more enlightened racial relations south of Mason-Dixon. They were, one infers from Cash, but expedient forms of southern *antimodernity* masquerading as "Progress," keeping intact all the while Old South mental habits—cherished myths and arrangements of white supremacy.

One may well question why Professor Cash's scholarly work holds premiere place in my analysis. For admittedly, the work's tenor and age would seem to mark it as anachronism. Indeed, Cash's analyses have been targeted by detractors during the entire existence of

The Mind of the South. Historians of the South such as C. Vann Woodward, V. O. Key Jr., and Paul Gaston have roundly denounced shortcomings of Cash's efforts. However, equally influential historians such as Fred Hobson, Bertram Wyatt-Brown, Richard King, and James C. Cobb have provided intriguingly nuanced accounts of the staying power and deep-structural achievements of *The Mind of the South.* In *Redefining Southern Culture: Mind and Identity in the Modern South,* Cobb writes:

> Cash's view of Reconstruction was strikingly similar to the prevailing popular and historical attitudes of his day—and, in that regard, strikingly dissimilar from most of the rest of his book. Yet Cash's now discredited treatment of Reconstruction notwithstanding, his analysis of its impact on the mind of the white South, that is, in Richard King's words, the creation of "a collective psycho-cultural entity—the South," was surely on or near the mark.[5]

In the year 2000, when America's primal, southern, and seemingly most newsworthy story centered on the State of South Carolina's refusal to lower the Confederate battle flag from atop its capitol, it would seem that Cash's work, rather than anachronistic, is usefully analytical and sadly prophetic. Which is to say, Cash was remarkably insightful when he allied southern resentment of Union occupation with Ireland's immemorial resentment of English power. For Cash was preeminently a psychocultural analyst of a unique order. He virtually intuited and then abundantly documented his thesis that the white South's abjection before an American "internal colonialism" produced a fiercely nationalistic regionalism south of Mason-Dixon. And this regionalism tended to set in stone, to hoist as flags and store in dry, shadowy attics racialistic attitudes and bizarre rituals of a *mind* always already made-up about incumbencies of framing the black body.

Why must we turn, and turn always again, to *The Mind of the South*?

Well, if Howard Zinn is correct, we read and reread Cash's book because in capturing the anticolonialist *resentiment* and psychocultural instrumentalities of "the South," Cash captured the "*essence* of the nation."[6] Zinn implicitly anticipated the current South Carolina controversy by decades when he points out that an "imagined" southern community of white supremacy—dedicated to preservation of old hypocrisies, xenophobia, racism, conservatism, and parodic elevation of white women to pedestals—serves as a resonant metonym for the United States as a whole. As Cobb notes, Cash was far less concerned about geographical nuances, and even stark differentiations at a level of regional functionalism, than he was interested in the unrelenting unanimity of what Cobb calls southern "commonalities of cultural terrain."[7] We might add, following Zinn, "national terrain." For, one might say Cash got the psycho-cultural commonalities of southern *resentiment* and racism absolutely "on the mark" not only for the Confederate states, but also for the United States at large. He captured, that is to say, the *mind* of America in providing a comprehensive analysis of what he called the *South.*

Ironically, of course, he and Malcolm X, John O. Killens, and all those fifty thousand people who recently converged on the capitol at Columbia, South Carolina, chanting for the lowering of the Confederate battle flag (and, subsequently, witnessed conservative Republicans like George Bush and John McCain virtually endorse southern racism for a chance at the United States presidency) are harmonious in their notation of the South's national cast in any global imaginary one can think. Cash indelibly captured the *mind of America* in his wonderfully troubling book. I deploy Cash because *The Mind of the South* seems to me coextensive with the demanding, fascinating, troubling complexities of my own southern revisionist project vis-à-vis black modernism and Booker T. Washington. I do not want to ignore Cash's detractors or successors. Indeed, they have informed my analyses. Still, it seems to me that Cash may have been not only prophetic in his realization of the deep-rootedness of the very worst of "southernness" in the United States, but also, perhaps, desperately and sadly proleptic in his own dispairing suicide, which occurred shortly after the release of his classic American book.

III

But a slight digression is required here on *the federal*. If it seems, by my concentration on the southern cast of national racial formation, I have ignored *Federalist* no. 10, this is simply because I believe the manifest content of what might be termed our "deep-structural national principles" often derives more from the local than the federal. Certainly, it is the southern local and regional that serve my own special interests here—namely "the mind of the South." *Federalist* no. 10, drafted by James Madison, does indeed establish the republican principles of private rights and property protection. A "republic," as opposed to a "democracy," according to Madison, is what the Constitution proposes. The Constitution holds, in fact, that the majority of citizens should be "voiced," as it were, by elected representatives—men qualified for governance by superior faculties for "acquiring property," unflagging devotion to a happy "Union," heroic in service to the "public good." Such national representative manhood's service will ensure that "great and aggregate interests [are] referred to the national, the *local and particular* to the State legislatures."[8]

The implicit motives of *Federalist* no. 10, therefore, despite their unifying nationalist aura, include the ensurance of "States Rights" read off as protection of private property and *local interests.* One might say peculiar *regional* interests are protected under provisions of *Federalist* no. 10, by a quite selective electorate, in combination with a bizarre construction of representation that enables black slaves to be tallied as three-fifths persons in matters of "representation." Fracture of the black body enables a sustainable southern mind.

In one sense, to argue there is a "southern mind" can be to minimize the reality that in colonial America *the federal* was constructed precisely to protect interests of a propertied, white, male citizenry everywhere. However, one of the most troublesome local issues for that citizenry was a whole "species of property" called slaves. And slaves were "lawful" property virtually everywhere in the precincts of colonial America. It was their ubiquity, in fact, that lent heft to states' rights, read off as southern "interests." And it was, I believe, the ubiquity of those interests that prompted the black twentieth-century writer John O. Killens to declare that America was all regionally southern, consisting of down south, up south, and out south.

Even beyond the gravity of *Federalist* no. 10, there are adequate distinguishing factors (as opposed to deep-structural national rhetorics of representation) for taking the South as a *peculiar space and state of mind.* It is these peculiarities that Cash delineates with engaging acumen. Such regional specificities serve me well for memoir and are indispensable to the analytics of the present discussion. Let me then boldly state there is nothing mythic, spuriously "authenticating," thoughtlessly or black-nationalistically essentialist in the assertion that *for the Black American majority of the nineteenth and early twentieth century, the mind of the South was critical to black personality, cultural, economic, and political formation*.

Of course, demographics and location alone do not allow us simply to "read off" a type of mystical folk essence among the black majority positioned in the South. But common sense suggests the *framing* of black being toward anything suitably called "modernity" has its primary locus south of Mason-Dixon. In Dixieland, black Americans had no choice but to take their stand . . . their performances framed in signifying relation to the mind of the South.

IV

Now, I know my regional claim may seem somewhat parlous, issuing as it does from a self-vested, middle-aged, black southerner by birth. What with the Great Migration of blacks to the North during the first decades of the twentieth century, immigration to the United States of blacks from (among other places) the Caribbean and Africa, and demographic shifts made by nonsouthern American blacks to wide open spaces of western territories such as Oklahoma, why should the mind of the South be privileged as the frame of black being? After all, mustn't we remember the extraordinary intellectual and social labor accomplished by what might be called a "black fugitive mobility" that brought the slave narrative into being . . . in the North? Mustn't we consider, as well, eighteenth- and nineteenth-century endeavors, on myriad fronts, by northern free blacks to stave off white attempts to colonize blacks, dispatching them "back to Africa"?

Certainly, my rationale for privileging the mind of the South does not ignore complicating demographic variables such as those just cited. It seems to me, however, despite such variables, the justification for privileging a southern frame of black American being is as expressively instrumental as the stirring strains of "We Shall Overcome" are as an international anthem of black liberation . . . everywhere, but most recently, of course, in South Africa. The song is, without doubt, the welling forth of black southern, grassroots organizational and political resolve forged in the framing economies—bodily and otherwise—of the South. Moreover, there is to be reckoned an inexhaustible expressive-cultural reservoir of black South experience that has played instrumentally modernist roles in the formulation of canons of such an international movement as *négritude*. This same expressive reservoir has served anticolonial psychoanalytical purposes of a genius like Franz Fanon in works such as *Black Skin, White Masks* and *The Wretched of the Earth*. Not only an earlier generation of West Indian intellectuals and culture workers such as C. L. R. James and Jacques Roumain looked to black intellectualism and black-South expressive cultural resonances, but also such recent artists/scholars as Kamau Braithwaite, Derek Walcott, and Paule Marshall.

Anxieties of intellectual influence and all-too-familiar bourgeois hankerings for black capitalist immigration to America, however, are finally less relevant with respect to the monumental significance of black-South experience than the metonymic black, southern performance of *modernity* in and of itself—and on native ground. It was preeminently this drama—body, mind, and soul—of black Americans coming up from slavery and aspiring toward modernity that shadowed the South in every performance, capturing global attention, exerting global political-expressive influence. The performance was most resonant on its own southern ground, one might claim, manifesting itself at its most august in the civil rights movement guided by the oratory and performative example of Dr. Martin Luther King Jr.

Black modernism is not only framed by the American South, but also is inextricable—as cognitive and somatic process of performing *blackness* out of or within tight spaces—from specific institutionalizations of human life below the Mason-Dixon. And the significance of this claim is not temporally confined to pre– or post–*Plessy v. Ferguson* operations of racism and the law. From the inscribed beginnings of the American Republic to the present day, it is the mind of the South (think, for but a moment, of Bill Clinton, Al Gore, Newt Gingrich, George W. Bush, and Trent Lott) that frames American being. "States' rights" as well as *Federalist* no. 10 offer examples of both geographical and class and economic grids of white power and white supremacist longing that are inseparable from the economic systems and implacable slave law of the American South.

"States' rights," of course, is an inherently racist compromise—one that ceded authority to a *region* to do essentially as it pleased with or against the black body. White southern agricultural profits are "states' rights" at the expense of the black body. In the 1990s, such rights have been redubbed "devolution," the return of power from federal to state governments. States' rights finally seem far less a beneficent "compromise" to ensure a more perfect union, than logical, long-term operators of white supremacy and profit. States' rights are as mortifying to the body of the "colored other" as we enter the twenty-first century as they were to black-South bodily interests two hundred years ago. Think, for but a moment, of state arrangements in today's prison-industrial complex, of which I shall have more to say later.

V

In the spirit of recall and summoned specters of both the critical and political past, I take up intellectual concerns, expressive themes, regional interests, and most importantly black expressive cultural practices that have occupied or haunted me for decades. My interest in revisiting uncannily familiar pleasures and horrors of the South has much to do with two questions that have continuously sallied forth in my recent attempts to create a memoir: *What precisely is the relationship of black-South performance to the mind of the South? What precisely is the relationship of black-South performance to black modernism?* Less academically: How does *blackness* walk the walk and talk the talk that leads the black majority to living in the light of a modern good life?

As I glance back now at some of my earlier criticism devoted to writers like Ralph Ellison, Richard Wright, James Baldwin, and Booker T. Washington from a millennial standpoint, much seems understated, hidden, or, too triumphal by half. I often conferred upon myself and my subjects far too great reward, or blame, for past accomplishments, or failures. I certainly overestimated—more than once—the sum of my subjects' purchase on the future. But, then, "black studies" once enjoyed enthusiastic youth in which brash overstatement, conative utterances, refusal to acknowledge even modest shortcomings, and playing unacknowledged legislators of the world seemed not only great fun but also essential to the survival of black studies. Much has changed. We are now more critical because we can afford to be; we are "established." Why, we even have our *Norton Anthology of African American Literature*!

More seriously, and in line with the requisite methodological self-consciousness, I confess I have been queried by more than one colleague about the memoiristic "framing" of the present discussion. As well, I have been sharply interrogated about why and how I have altered or "compromised" an interpretation of Booker T. Washington, modernism, and my family's black southern life as presented in my 1987 monograph *Modernism and the Harlem Renaissance*. Under such interrogation, a critic can always fall back upon "the elders," who are normally "great (black) men"—those who have, in the course of their careers, sharply altered perspectives and prose surrounding the conundrum of "race" in America.

For example, W. E. B. Du Bois made a seismic shift from his youthful commitment to social scientific "objectivity" as solution to the American race problem, to a radically black separatist proposal drafted in his seventies. Why did Du Bois shift? In his "autobiography of a race concept" titled *Dusk of Dawn,* he says the motivation was his own belated discovery of Freud and Marx. Objective "facts," Du Bois suggests, have no effect in the face of deeply rooted, white psychological prejudices and economic arrangements of dominance and subordination they sustain.

In my own present instance of methodological change, I can offer only the following belated riposte: "Who knew the adoption of psychoanalysis would offer a radically refigured comprehension of Tuskegee and its founder?" Such a riposte would be flat-footedly true, yet disingenuous. For in genuine earnest, my return to the scene of Tuskegee and Booker T. Washington has as much to do with anxiety as with ethnography . . . or epiphany. The anxiety, as already hinted, has to do with *ghosts.* Booker T. Washington is long dead; my own father more recently so. The alliance between Washington's Tuskegee and my father's accomplishments always seemed a point of honor, especially when I wrote *Modernism and the Harlem Renaissance* . . . a time when my father's corpse was a daily and nightly specter. Washington and my father built institutions to serve the black majority. Both were "practical" men; doers, not dreamers. However, I have garnered more information in a decade; visited my father's grave and spoken with him, more than once since *Modernism* . . . always seeking to capture dim aspects, aspirations of "Houston Sr." that were less salient a decade ago. I have learned his dream-driven idealism—belatedly. My dad wanted to know Grand Opera, sample Great Literature, attain Culture. Most significantly, he sustained (always) a virtual faith that if he made the right culture-cultivating moves he would be called to courts of earthly, refined (read "white") power on grounds of total equality.

How can I claim to know these things?

Well, writing memoir can . . . at least for me . . . include interviews with a mother who in her eighties, possesses twenty-twenty vision and a mind and memory to match. She knew my father "when." . . . Through all the time he was alive and aspiring to "culture." She speaks now of his "exceptionalism" in her world, how remarkable his quest was for a black man born deeply inside what Du Bois in describing black-South folk terrain called "the veil," how anomalous his aspirations seemed to her in the person of a man of my father's impoverished southern background.

One significant (dare one say "methodological"?) aspect of memoir, then, is that one never *stops* re-membering. We especially remember those whose example, willy-nilly, conditions all we do and become. There is, I believe, a continuous memoiristic imperative to the formation of black male subjectivity in the United States of America. But I do not mean by this, a high-black-comedic mode of outrageous autobiographical lies. Rather, what I have in mind . . . my notion of where the black methodological and memoiristic coalesce, or collide, depending upon one's point of view . . . is exactly captured by the scholar Patricia Yaeger's resonant question: "What does it mean to turn [dead] bodies into rhetoric?"[9]

VI

In her courageous and brilliant essay, Yaeger writes as follows: "The ventriloquism we lend to the dead, the tropes we clothe them in, can have the power to re-dress their bodies, to speak volumes. . . . [But] how do we identify the proper tone, the proper images, for holding—for awakening—someone else's bodily remains?" (228). Yaeger's compelling exploration of writer-critics' responsibilities to *the dead*—responsibilities spanning economic, pedagogical, rhetorical, political dimensions of we who "circulate" essays of injury and pain for a living—helped me answer methodological questions about memoir, re-vision, and "poetics of another story."

Now, this is not simply a way of saying that "trauma studies" gave me convenient loopholes where I could take refuge and fire away at questions of method and revision. No, it is rather to say Yaeger's astute realizations and cogently polemical insights gave me a looser space in which to work.

Yaeger convinces me utterly that some writer-critics encounter, imagine, *image* specters—"dead subjects"—far more *nervously,* and hence, far more exactingly than others. "Bodily remains" require special handling in our "entrepreneurial space of academic play" (231). Yaeger writes: "[T]he dangers implicit in the rhetoricization of a black man's body can have material effects . . . [because] the depersonification of African Americans is an ongoing, repetitive stratagem within American history" (233). Her statement is clarified and amplified by the author's politically radical critique of "academic play":

> In calling out to the specter we encounter a new kind of nightmare: not the gothic terror of being haunted by the dead, but the greater terror *of not being haunted,* of ceasing to feel the weight of past generations in one's bones. That is, the words we use to hold the dead, to call out to them, are too porous, too leaky. . . . I want some portion of this weight to descend on the reader's body, to create a burdensome space for thinking about the relationship between representational melancholy and political praxis. (236)

Here we have it, then.

Far too sanguine about the "trauma" of my father's being-in-the-world—his necessarily vexed relationship as a black male southerner to "modernism"—I allied his corpse with that of Booker T. Washington. It was so convenient for my ludic, academic claims upon the past to do so. I fashioned my father as an institution builder, ever anxious to "protect and serve." Adopting, as Yaeger might define it, the "trope of Booker T. Washington," I evacuated more nuanced "contexts" of my father's own signal corpse . . . and he could not contest my claims; he is the "subject who can not speak back." No matter, though . . . because my father's was a far more complex "South" than I had ever imagined, till now . . . and I am becoming that "South" . . . I am becoming him, striving to find proper performative "images" to connect my living and the dead . . . to make distinctions between the "famous" and infamous injury to the black dreamer who was my progenitor.

What implications for method exist in all of this?

I find my readers (far, far too grandiose a phrase, of course, for the handful who care whether I write or not) seem intensely more "cheerful" and braced when they hear that no matter what horror and death were occasioned by being merely black and in the South, robust, energetic black men like Washington and my father still were able to avoid "contagion," to strive, laugh at life's little ironies, and survive. Such regional characterization from me makes me, for the reader, a black avatar of optimism—a latter-day and triumphal personal earnest that liberalism's implicit commitment to doing the right thing is real, and indeed embodied in my very black authorship in America. Such characterization, of course, burnishes the dread reality of black majority dying. It ameliorates horror through black male figural imaginings . . . among ghosts.

Two further observations from Yaeger locate my concern for revision, my answer to the question "Why have you changed your mind/assessment?" Alluding to the summoning of the dead in *The Odyssey,* Yaeger writes: "It would seem that the dead can only speak when they partake of the things [blood] of this world. . . . [T]he trace of the specter's speech resides neither in the dead's wished-for presence nor in their oblivion, but in their inevitable hybridity. They must be fed on the life blood, the figures of the present, if they are to speak" (238). This is a methodologically loaded claim, of course, implying one is honorably and materially bound to find proper, concrete images, tropes, and figures before one may realize the potential of the dead—their instructional *scenes.*

An observation on the aptness of "instructional scenes" is the final site I wish to visit in Yaeger's fine essay. Only the specter, invoked and made present by the figure of our imagining, can lead us toward the "new," the revolutionary, a modernity of consciousness impelled by the interests of the black majority: "Marx suggests that 'new problems and paradigms' depend upon the dead's borrowed names. This means that revolutionary thinking is 'never free of anxiety'; or, in Derrida's haunting of Marx, 'conjuration is anxiety from the moment it calls upon death to invent the quick and to enliven the new, to summon the presence of what is not yet there'" (247).

I turn and return to proximate figures of my father and Booker T. Washington. Now, I do so for purposes of distinction. I ask: "How do two dead black male bodies haunt a context that seems the same, but actually is dramatically fractured by differential possibilities of movement?" I live in a haunted place. Thus I must come politically and memorially to terms with ghosts.

VII

Had I not previously entered a field of "entrepreneurial academic play," the discussion that follows would not be a haunting of myself. On the other hand, had I not entered what is still a very radically unlevel academic playing field, who would have asked questions or challenged my revisionary performance . . . or expected, from me, perhaps deathly titillating meta-accounts of my own black male "performativity"? The question then arises: "What's in the *names* titling black books actually written by ourselves, as black males?" Here is the double bind, I think, of being black, male, and *not dead* . . . even accommodatingly "socially dead," in the phrase Orlando Patterson provides in his definition of slavery as social death.[10]

I hazard as a hypothesis only that black male subjectivity in modern formation is not only an interrogation of the bodies of the dead but also an endless stigmatizing trauma of the revisionary . . . which is not without its pleasures of all-American and endless "circulation." This "pleasure," of course, is of a qualified sort: being alive, engaged in political, inscriptive praxis that makes "new" generations feel the weight of the *progressive dead* in the very marrow of their bones is sweet only *sometimes.* For such work is always allied to black bodies on death row, in open-air homicide zones of neglected city spaces, or monitoring T cell counts that fall and fall and fall. Memoir and Booker T. Washington—figuratively fashioned in the analytical mode of psychoanalysis—can bring, I think, light and enlightenment to such zones of black disappearance. What fitter corridor is there, after all, through the memorial house of black (so often male) ghosts than Booker T. and the American South? Even in earlier encounters, memoir (including those black-and-white photographs of my family) was at the very heart of *Modernism and the Harlem Renaissance* . . . disguised, I now admit, as colored "promise" from within and dictated by very "tight places." My earlier encounter with Thanatos was telling, perhaps, but not nearly (to recur to Yaeger) *nervous enough.* It quite simply did not allow me to "figure" modernism in respect to black majority interests in the most weightily haunting, fluidly mobile ways imaginable. And now, in the present, black male death is everywhere, everywhere around us.

But we shall return in the course of the present discussion to clear life-and-death matters more than once. For analytic purposes now, though, I want to register as astutely as possible the variations on *modernism* marking the following pages. A definitional interlude is needed.

The transformed and transforming complex of experience and innovation—cultural contact, exchange, and possibilities—that I call *black modernism* has, for me, both primary and secondary definitions. Primarily, *black modernism* signifies the achievement of a life-enhancing and empowering public sphere mobility and the economic solvency of the black majority. At this principal order of definition, *black modernism* is coextensive with a black citizenship that entails documented mobility (driver's license, passport, green card, social security card) and access to a decent job at a decent rate of pay. A central right and incumbency of black modernism, as well, is the vote. The black modernism of the civil rights movement was most clearly marked and broadcast by its insistent public sphere marchers (mobility) aimed at securing jobs, freedom, the vote for the black majority.

To designate a modernism as "secondary" does not, for me, imply a chronology so much as a ranking of significance, indeed, a shading of influence and effect. What I call "mulatto modernism" defines a gospel and dynamics of *uplift*. For me, "mulatto modernism" is race- and class-inflected along a distinctive axis of representation. Bourgeois, middle-class individualism, vestimentary and hygienic impeccability, oratorical and double-conscious "race pride," and protonationalism are defining characteristics of "mulatto modernism." Like the term "mulatto" itself, the modernism it suggests is a project in ambivalence. For example, claims to possibilities of superior representational and racial-stock capabilities of the hue *black* are predicated on endless rhetorical rehearsals (in ambivalence) of how progressively "lighter and lighter" the "race" is becoming. A certain heroic and ironic absurdity, thus, marks "mulatto modernism" such as Frederick Douglass's claim in his 1845 *Narrative* that illicit white male sexual intercourse with black women slaves in the South is threatening to transform the "sons of Ham" into a new and unenslaved southern "nation." Such irony not only implies ambivalence but also gestures toward a certain species of "favored nation" eugenics that is more intriguingly problematic than, say, assimilation. A chief tenet of "mulatto modernism" is "uplift," the translation of individual, bourgeois, class achievement into doctrinal and pedagogical imperatives for the black masses. However, given the odd eugenic "doublings" of this secondary modernism, rather than being uplifting for the black majority the process often deploys precisely the "darkness" of the majority as the necessary, preeminent, and sufficient representational sign of its own *modernity.*

Du Bois's "Talented Tenth," even in biblical significations of the "talent," entails, without seeming equivocation, an "untalented," infertile, bereft nine-tenths—that is to say, the black majority. Nevertheless, without such precursor *modernisms* as the mulatto, a deathly silence may well have doomed ten-tenths of blackness to American extinction, a shrouded and veiled termination of "the race," as it were.

Finally, there is the phrase "Afro-modernity," which I use to signify the general effects of African, African diasporic, and Afro-American people's "stride toward freedom," their move toward a cosmopolitan mobility of citizenship, work, cultural reclamation and production that enhance the lives of a black majority globally conceived. "Afro-modernity" might be considered as a project in style, resistance, organization, art, literacy, and spirituality that surfaces from, say, Atlantic depths and holds, stretching from at least the fifteenth century to phantasmagorical transformations of South Africa in the 1990s. The preeminent dynamics of Afro-modernity are the "search" for Africa, the query "What is Africa to me?"

In the discussion that follows I turn to psychoanalysis and social psychology in combination with observations from the world of performance studies to address matters of black modernism. These are new disciplinary departures for me—a me who is still alive, reasonably well, black, and male in the academic world. I welcome responses from masters of the fields. In the pages immediately following, I am drawn back, via dynamics of Booker T. Washington's endless haunting of any Afro-modernism we can yet imagine. And my first task is to define "performance."

VIII

For me, "performance" is human activity engaged in by an agent who is both conscious of and seeking to satisfy some standard of achievement, a standard that may not be precisely articulated. I do not mean by performance, therefore, either a virtuosic display of technical skills, as in a spirited rendering of the *Rach Three*. Nor do I intend even the most exacting presentations of scripted characterization, for example, Laurence Fishburne in *Othello*. The performance I have in mind is human activity that *re*-presents a potential, remembered, or ideal model. This *model* constitutes the performance's implicit *frame*. Social psychology's relationship to my notions of performance and framing is best captured in the writings of Erving Goffman.[11] Drawing on Gregory Bateson's observation that play can be seen as nonserious activity modeled on its serious complement, Goffman offers the following definition of frames as "situations . . . built up in accordance with principles of organization which govern events—at least social ones—and our subjective involvement in them" (10–11).

"*Frame*," says Goffman, "is the word I use to refer to such of these basic elements [or 'principles of organization'] as I am able to identify" (155). In his work, Goffman also draws on the vocabulary of film studies, employing the term "strip" to refer to "any arbitrary cut from the stream of ongoing happenings . . . as seen from the perspective of those . . . involved in sustaining an interest in them" (155). Of course, the multiple frames of a filmstrip in motion produce a *scene*.

As sustained, subjective interactions layered with ongoing, serious happenings, *frames* are spaces where cultural ideals are performed by human beings in commerce. For example, what the anthropologist Victor Turner calls the "liminal" middle stage of a rite of passage is a frame.[12] It is, in fact, an initiatory and performative frame for shedding masks of innocence, acquiring language and lore of the tribe, and exiting the frame into a new social status.

For the present discussion, I want to assert that the framing mind of the South has been and remains a liminal zone, a middle passage of the imagination, a space of performance, a series of peculiar "strips" of interactive behavior where *blackness* has played or performed toward the *scene* of modernity. Elsewhere, I have written of a "black (w)hole" performativity of black American life that has given birth to a quite extraordinary expressivity—blackness in motion toward modernity.[13] This "black (w)hole" might be thought of as a frame within the framing mind of the South. Rhetorically, what the writer Henry Louis Gates Jr. calls "signifying" constitutes a black framing and performance of language within, around, and in the interstices of dominant discourses.[14] Such rhetorical masking is, of course, coextensive with doubling, reflexive dynamics of a poet such as Paul Laurence Dunbar whose black "mask" "grins and lies" as reaction formation to a dominant, white, and subjugating discourse: "Why should the world be overwise? / Nay, we wear the mask."[15]

The negotiating frames for blackness—as with all human social interaction considered under the prospect of social psychology—are *always* performative. Rhetorically, expressively, cognitively, psychologically, kinesthetically, such frames of negotiation are complex *re*-presentations conditioned by cultural ideals or models. Goffman says, in the passage I use as an epigraph to this chapter, "when we come to be able to manage a real routine we are able to do this in part because of 'anticipatory socialization,' having already been schooled [framed, as it were] in the reality that is just coming to be real for us."[16]

The framing of *blackness* by black Americans in the United States is always, at least in part, a defense against clear liabilities of the black American body being legally and juridically *framed*. By this,

I mean that performativity of an elaborate cast is deployed as defense against the summary sentencing of *blackness* to the outlands: enslavement, peonage, tenantry, urban ghetto banishment, differential mandatory sentencing to long-term imprisonment, death row.

Only the *scene* that results from articulation and the memorial offices of long, black-South framing—manifold critically remembered black performances—forestalls black permanent exile from the human race. Booker T. Washington's life and work during Reconstruction and its New South aftermath intriguingly inaugurate, I believe, a specific black-South dynamics of being, framing, and performance toward black modernism critical for any adequate understanding of Afro-modernity. Washington's 1901 opus *Up from Slavery* seems just the right text to analyze under the sign "performance." Returning to the scene of this classic autobiography enables me, of course, to revisit . . . to converse once more with the restless, haunting black fathers who refuse to allow a black southerner, critic, scholar, or son easily to avoid tight places.

IX

Following extensive narration of the momentous success of his 1895 speech to the Atlanta Cotton States and International Exposition in *Up from Slavery,* Washington elaborates his metaphor of "public speaking" that commences at almost exactly the midpoint of his autobiography, in a chapter titled "Two Thousand Miles for a Five-Minute Speech." By the time we have read the narrator's exultant account of his Atlanta address, we are firmly persuaded that the boss of Tuskegee is a "master" of public forms of expression. He regularly speaks, we are informed, to wildly enthusiastic reviews. Yet, three-quarters of the way toward the conclusion of his autobiography, Washington writes as follows:

> People often ask me if I feel nervous before speaking, or else they suggest that, since I speak so often, they suppose that I get used to it. In answer to this question I have to say that I always suffer intensely from nervousness before speaking. More than once, just

> before I was to make an important address, this nervous strain has been so great that I have resolved never again to speak in public. I not only feel nervous before speaking, but after I have finished I usually feel a sense of regret, because it seems to me as if I had left out of my address the main thing and the best thing that I had meant to say. (148)

The nervousness Washington describes can accurately be described not simply as mild discomfort. A more exacting characterization would in fact be "social anxiety," a specific phobia defined as follows by the fourth edition of the *Diagnostic and Statistical Manual of Mental Disorders (DSM-IV):*[17]

> The essential feature of Social Phobia is a marked and persistent fear of social performance situations in which embarrassment may occur. Exposure to the social or performance situation almost invariably provokes an immediate anxiety response. This response may take the form of a situationally bound or situationally predisposed Panic Attack. Although adolescents and adults with this disorder recognize their fear is excessive or unreasonable this may not be the case with children. Most often, the social or performance situation is avoided, although it is sometimes endured with dread. The diagnosis is appropriate only if the avoidance, fear, or anxious anticipation of encountering the social or performance situation interferes with the person's daily routine, occupational functioning, or social life, or if the person is markedly distressed about having the phobia. (411)

This sounds remarkably like a fear of "tight places" to me.

Phrases that stand out in the *DSM-IV* are "endured with dread" and "panic attack." Here is what the manual says of "panic attacks": "The essential feature of a Panic Attack is a discrete period of intense fear or discomfort that is accompanied by at least 4 of 13 somatic or cognitive symptoms. The attack has a sudden onset and builds to a peak rapidly . . . and is often accompanied by a sense of imminent danger or impending doom and an urge to escape" (394). Symptoms are derealization (feeling of unreality) or depersonalization (being detached from oneself); fear of dying; parathesia (numbness or tingling sensations); chills or hot flushes.

On the basis of *DSM-IV,* it seems that Washington, by his own account, suffered panic attacks as regular occurrences in his social phobia of public speaking. Furthermore, it seems audience expectation—especially insofar as the audience consisted of white men positioned to give approbation and substantial philanthropic sums to Washington and Tuskegee—precipitated such attacks. We listen as Washington describes his first visit—in Richmond, Virginia, capital of the Confederacy—to the Honorable J. L. M. Curry, general agent of the Peabody and Slater philanthropic foundations that contributed handsomely to black educational institutions such as Tuskegee. Washington writes: "I shall never forget the first time I met him. . . . I had heard so much about him. When I went into his presence, trembling because of my youth and inexperience, he took me by the hand so cordially, and spoke such encouraging words, and gave me such helpful advice regarding the proper course to pursue, that I came to know him then, and I have known him ever since, as a high example of one who is constantly and unselfishly at work for the betterment of humanity" (121). This trembling encounter between an ex-slave who is now head of a black southern school and an ex-general commences with anxious dread . . . followed by reassuring physical contact, "encouraging" words, and monitory advice that lead to calm confidence.

A panic attack is thus ameliorated in a face-to-face ritual of patronage. Washington's "performance"—despite trembling anxiety—seems to win the day. The questions for readers of *Up from Slavery* are: Why is Washington so filled with panic on occasions of public performance? Why is it useful to interpret the narrator's social phobia as anything other than the type of acute nervousness most of us feel when called upon to stage an important meeting or to speak publicly?

The simplest answer is an analytical one: we must attend to Washington's panic, phobia, and performance anxiety because they are manifest symptoms of psychological dimensions of his autobiography that have seldom (if ever) been considered by cultural and literary studies. In a probing essay titled "Psychology and Afro-American Biography," the scholar Arnold Rampersad asserts: "I believe it is fair to say that, far from being influenced by psychology, black biography has kept a vast distance between itself and that discipline. If one looks at even the most acclaimed books in the field, one sees hardly any attempt to link the art of biography to what I call—if only in provocation—the science of psychoanalysis."[18] Rampersad goes on to say, "A published psychological study of a black leader is an act of courage in itself—so entrenched is the opposition to such work" (9). Rampersad further postulates that black resistance to psychoanalytical criticism stems from both an overprotective "racial loyalty" and a parochial aversion to Western "science."

Given the signal achievement of Rampersad's own brilliant two-volume biography of Langston Hughes—a work rich in psychoanalytical insight—his methodological injunctions seem worth heeding. As he reports, there is no use shying away from the symptomatic or psychologically evidential in the life and work of black leaders such as Booker T. Washington. For the "truth" yielded by psychoanalytical attention to uplift epics such as *Up from Slavery* will always eventually be revealed. And what a fascinating psychological truth it is in the case of Washington's performing "I."

X

Washington's story begins in the physical absence of the white father—the white man who did the "work" of impregnating his mother but whose identity remains unknown. The boy Booker is marked from birth by what W. E. B. Du Bois poetically called the "red stain of bastardy" so familiar as a cultural marker in the economics of slavery—the notorious doctrine of *partus sequitur ventrem,* where the status of the child is determined by the status of the mother.[19] The black mother is all-in-all as provider. She labors, nevertheless, under the burden of illicit sexuality: an implicit "licentiousness" inferred, paradoxically, from the "bastardy" of her son, whose "legitimate" white father makes himself a secret. Nineteenth-century American racial science considered licentiousness a fixed, biological trait of black American women. In his autobiography, Washington writes: "I have seen the statement made lately, by one who claims to know what he is talking about, that, taking the whole Negro race into account, ninety per cent of the Negro women are not virtuous. There never was a baser falsehood uttered concerning a race or a statement made that was less capable of being proved by actual facts" (164). There is a black stepfather who comes into the boy's life before slavery officially ends with the signing at Appomattox. But this stepfather seems to have been scarcely more than a labor broker in Booker's and his older brother's lives. When the mother and her two sons leave Virginia and join the stepfather in West Virginia, the nine-year-old Booker is signed on by his stepfather to labor in the salt works and coal mines of Malden. The boy becomes a sort of freedman's David Copperfield. The squalor of his neighborhood, where the laboring classes live, appalls the young Washington. Dirt, litter, contagion all characterize this laboring-class life in the raw.

The stepfather is never portrayed as affectionate, caring, or paternal—he confiscates all the wages earned by Booker and his older brother John. Can we be surprised then that schooling and educational advancement—ideals circulating in the postbellum air breathed by many southern freedmen—appealed to Booker? Here was an alternative to virtual impressment in the packing of salt barrels and dragging of heavy loads of coal in lightless mines of West Virginia. To this point—the age of eleven or twelve years—Booker's life was certainly "dysfunctional" with respect to human liberty, fatherly affection, maternal "purity," "dignified" labor, possibilities of a clean, well-lighted place of habitation, and even a full name of his own—complete with middle initial and legitimate surname:

> From the time when I could remember anything, I had been called simply "Booker." Before going to school it had never occurred to me that it was needful or appropriate to have an additional name. . . . By the time the occasion came for the enrolling of my name, an idea occurred to me which I thought would make me equal to the situation; and so, when the teacher asked me what my full

> name was I calmly told him "Booker Washington," as if I had been called by that name all my life; and by that name I have since been known. Later in life I found that my mother had given me the name of "Booker Taliaferro" soon after I was born. . . . I revived it, and my full name "Booker Taliaferro Washington." (47)

Framing the dysfunctional absence and lack of "Booker's" life in its first instances is the mind of the South, manifested in an elaborate, brutal, profitable system of chattel slavery. Born the illegitimate (nameless) child of a white father who, one speculates, followed the "class privilege" of his slave ownership in impregnating the boy's mother, Booker was left simply to "tumble up" in the world the slaveholders made. His home was a dirt-floor cabin that provided neither shelter nor comfort. And the general white policing and surveillance of the southern slave system virtually foreclosed any *black public*, or *manifestly free movement*. Unrestricted and unmonitored travel were out of the question for the black-South body. Slave law specifically forbade not only public movement, but also personal development—even acquisition or teaching of skills of reading and writing.

Goffman calls such calculated, severe, and mortifying systems of human framing as black slavery "total institutions."[20] He includes prisons and asylums in the class of such institutions. "Booker" was framed by the total institution of his autobiography's title, namely *slavery*. The mark—distinctiveness of soma or body—that defined the inmates of slavery was none other than *blackness*.

XI

In his comprehensive and passionate history of slave law during the colonial period, titled *In the Matter of Color,* legal scholar and jurist Leon Higginbotham writes: "Only against nonwhites did colonial society feel it could use anything and everything—the legal structure, the militia, even armed private citizens—to keep human beings in a submissive state."[21] Higginbotham commences his work with seventeenth-century Virginia statutes that provide a characterization of the black slave's legal status that obtained in the South for the next 180 years. He writes as follows:

> If blacks could not leave the owner's plantation without a certificate, their mobility was destroyed; if blacks could not carry arms, the potential to resist was reduced. And, if blacks could be whipped [even unto death] for lifting up a hand against any Christian—regardless of the provocation—then the dehumanization process was complete, because blacks were legally precluded from responding in a manner thought normal for whites or most other human beings. (39)

The body's natural "color" was converted into a legalized mark of oppression. There was, in the total institution called slavery, an *epidermalization* of oppression. Skin color—in combination with facial features and hair texture—became southern grounds for maintenance of the ideological and economic project of White Supremacy. And when "freedom" arrived at the end of the Civil War—the ceremonial, military abolition of chattel slavery—the South was not without its totalizing alternatives. Convict lease labor, peonage, sharecropping, and contract and vagrancy laws requiring "freed" blacks to prove within ten days of summons that they were self-supporting, or face imprisonment; these were southern norms. It seems more literal than metaphorical in such instances, therefore, to agree with scholars and writers who assert that "slavery" indeed continued "after the war." And the mark of Reconstruction's innovative mechanisms of White Supremacy remained skin color, *blackness*.

There can be little wonder, then, that Washington's *Up from Slavery* codes the world in binary terms of *black* and *white*. Given the total institutional strategies and arrangements of southern slavery, law, and labor practices, it should surprise no one that Washington's life story also codes its world in terms of those who have (own, possess financial resources, oversee money and property) and those who don't (are owned as property, are indictable as bereft of capital reserves).

Washington's mind and body were framed by a southern world whose ruling proposition, as a later black writer would succinctly state it, was that "black is a terrible color with which to be born into the world."[22] In postbellum Malden, West Virginia, however, "Booker" turned the southern system of black epidermalization and white derogation on its head. And he did so through strategic performance. Having convinced his stepfather to allow him to spend a portion of each workday at school, Booker is confronted with the necessity to "get ahead of himself," to alter the very time in which he exists. *Up from Slavery* records:

> [Since] I had to work till nine o'clock, and the school opened at nine, I found myself in a difficulty. School would always be begun before I reached it, and sometimes my class had recited. To get around this difficulty I yielded to a temptation for which most people, I suppose, will condemn me, but since it is a fact, I might as well state it. . . . There was a large clock in a little office in the [building where the salt] furnace [was located]. This clock, of course, all the hundred or more workmen depended upon to regulate their hours of beginning and ending the day's work. I got the idea that the way for me to reach school on time was to move the clock hands from half-past eight up to the nine o'clock mark. (45–46)

Booker distances himself—through time's manipulation—from the "hundred or more workmen." He then travels to a site of black literacy, where he bestows upon himself a proper name, complete with middle initial. Booker literally alters time and status as he moves away from the laboring classes, from restrictions of common black-South experience and the posttraumatic stress of slavery. Temporally, he is on his way performatively "up." Spatially, he soon performs his way into the very house of the white owners:

> While at work [in the lightless coal mines where he hears talk of Hampton Normal and Agricultural Institute], I heard of a vacant position in the household of General Lewis Ruffner, the owner of the salt-furnace and coal-mine. Mrs. Viola Ruffner, the wife

> of General Ruffner, was a 'Yankee' woman from Vermont. Mrs. Ruffner had a reputation all through the vicinity for being very strict with her servants, and especially with the boys who tried to serve her. Few of them had remained with her more than two or three weeks. . . . I decided I would rather try Mrs. Ruffner's house than remain in the coal-mine. . . . I was hired at a salary of $5 per month. (51–52)

A "Yankee" white woman and a temporally anxious, spatially ambitious southern black boy come together in the general-owner's house. They represent, I believe, iconic figures in the psychosocial framing of black-South experience: white "vacancy" of the legitimate father intriguingly reconfigured by Washington's black "occupancy."

XII

The all-American caricature of the "Yankee" schoolmarm paints her as a crabbed, aged, old maid fiddling with books, cats, and outcasts. W. J. Cash captures this stereotype when he writes in *The Mind of the South* as follows: "Generally horsefaced, bespectacled, and spare of frame, she was, of course, no proper intellectual, but at best a comic character, at worst a dangerous fool, playing with explosive forces which she did not understand" (140). Contrary to stereotype and caricature, however, the "Yankee" womanhood that made its way South after the war was often young, literate, predominantly white, and in the age range of twenty to thirty years old. Washington's prizewinning biographer, Louis Harlan, notes that such women were often quite physically attractive.[23] Writing (with perhaps too much manly enthusiasm) Harlan describes the personnel of General Samuel Chapman Armstrong's Hampton Institute: "For classroom teachers, considered essentially a feminine occupation, Armstrong plucked the very flowers of New England. He lured southward maiden ladies of exquisite sensibility and devotion to genteel culture and self-improvement, womanly women, often very pretty, for the young general [thirty-seven years of age when Booker T. Washington first encountered him] had an eye for the fair sex"

(62). Here, "Yankee" with respect to womanhood scarcely signifies crabbed unattractiveness, and "maidenhood" suggests innumerable prospects with respect to sexuality and its southern psychological and physical entailments. Harlan writes: "If Mrs. Ruffner represented to the young mulatto houseboy a godsend to save him from the heavy labor of the furnaces and mines, so must he have been a godsend to her. She was married to a man almost twenty years older than she, far from her childhood home, and rejected by his children" (42). Viola Ruffner was shy, introverted, nervous, reclusive, and "frequently," in the judgment of one of her nephews by marriage, "hysterical." She and Booker T. Washington became intimates in the household of the white owner General Ruffner—a man incapacitated by an injury suffered when he attempted to calm a racial dispute between Ku Klux Klansmen and armed black men in Malden.

The rituals into which Booker T. and Viola Ruffner entered included her instruction to the adolescent in reading and writing but also in an implicitly obsessive "purification": "She wanted everything kept clean about her," writes Washington. Mrs. Ruffner teaches Booker not only to "sweep," but to be nearly fanatical in his desire for system, order, maintenance, fastidiously laundered vestments and whitewashed odorless dwelling places. Harlan comments: "Booker must have noticed a difference in smell, appearance, and feel between the Ruffner way of life on the hill and the way the common white and black people lived down below. . . . Washington learned so well the New England message of cleanliness and good order that for the rest of his life he could never see bits of paper strewn in a house or in the street without wanting to pick them up at once. He could never see a yard cluttered with trash without a restless urge to clean it" (43). What I believe Viola Ruffner and Booker T. Washington enacted—within the framing house of the framing mind of the white general—was an intimacy of purity and danger.

The symbolic anthropologist Mary Douglas suggests in her classic study *Purity and Danger* that any society's definition of "dirt" (danger) is merely an irreplaceable category for the achievement of order: dirt is "matter out of place."[24] Decontamination and purity depend very much upon ritual acts of sweeping or cleaning up the taboos of "dirt." Such work can only be effected by the risky coming into proximity—even the symbolic and "magically" protected handling and negotiation—of the tabooed, the outlawed. I think in the dwelling place of the general-owner, Booker found his own ritual purification from *blackness*—discovered, indeed, through a "sweeping" intimacy with Mrs. Ruffner, possibilities for an entirely new order of owner-class arrangements of body and mind.

Metaphorically, Viola Ruffner oversaw the robust, ambitious black adolescent's bathing in the light and purity of "Yankee" womanist intimacy. It seems impossible to ignore the sexual overtones of such an encounter—whether these overtones became moments of actual physical contact, or remained only desire sublimated into joint rituals of "sweeping," we cannot say. But we do know dysfunctional, laboring-class *blackness* yields in Booker's everyday life to knowledge of and desire for ordered, domestic rounds of clean linens, properly set dinner tables, odorless rooms, the brotherhood of soap and water, and light-skinned women as the most companionable and intimate of helpmeets.

The Yankee woman imperatives of this change of Booker's consciousness and his performative escape from the "I" of black-South derogation are reinforced, of course, by Washington's "entrance examination" to Hampton Institute. His admission is overseen by one of General Armstrong's "maiden ladies of exquisite sensibility," named Miss Mary Mackie. Miss Mackie is the white head teacher of the institute. The examination, as all readers of *Up from Slavery* recall, consists of "sweeping," repetitive, obsessive cleaning of the recitation room of the main academic building:

> I knew I could sweep, for Mrs. Ruffner had thoroughly taught me how to do that when I lived with her.
>
> I swept the recitation-room three times. Then I got a dusting-cloth and I dusted it four times. All the woodwork around the walls, every bench, table, and desk, I went over four times with my dusting cloth. . . . When . . . [Miss Mackie] was unable to find one

> bit of dirt on the floor, or a particle of dust on any furniture, she quietly remarked, "I guess you will do to enter this institution." (56–57)

Again, we are party as readers to a ritual of "occupancy." Booker is permitted "in" by the Yankee woman, a "womanly woman," to be sure. Later in his Hampton career, Miss Mackie invites Booker to return in advance of fall term to help her sweep Hampton's buildings.

(When I delivered an earlier and less elaborated version of this analysis, an excellent black undergraduate raised his hand at the end of the presentation and said: "Sir, where is all of that 'sweeping' you are talking about? We read this book in my honors seminar and we didn't see any of that." At, literally, a soul-food eatery in Georgia later that evening, I asked one of my excellent, age-group colleagues why the undergraduate had not "seen" the sweeping, and she answered: "Because he has never listened to the blues." To wit, here is Willie's Reed's "Dreaming Blues":

> Excuse me, mama, for knocking at your room
> If I can't be your sweeper, let me be your broom.

And Willie Baker's "Rag Baby" blues:

> Yonder she goes, with a broom in her hand
> Sweep me off, for another man.

The magnificent Robert Johnson intones in his classic "I Believe I'll Dust My Broom":

> I'm going to get up in the morning, I believe I'll dust my broom
> Because then the black man you been loving, girl friend can get my room.

Finally, the "Divine One," Sarah Vaughan has to be heard singing the line "Love is a second-hand broom." I believe the excellent undergraduate's honors seminar would have done well if it had had the blues.)

I consider the sweeping moments of interracial cleaning *framed rituals.* In both the Ruffner and Mackie instances, they are outside of and interlayered with ordinary southern time. Taboos are suspended. We have a form of liminal or transitional instruction as Booker is transfigured from dirty *blackness* into "Booker Taliaferro Washington"—a "New Negro," ahead of his time with respect to "civilization," and white womanist intimacy.

(On two separate speaking occasions subsequent to my encounter with the honors undergraduate, speakers of Italian stole up to me and asked if I knew that language. I do not. So they informed me of the currency of "sweeping" in Italian. *Scopare* is an active verb for the vernacular forbidden, the "F" word in Italian. *Scopare* is open in its double signification. As one informant suavely put it: "I sweep the floor and then, I sweep my wife." I found the point very well made.)

XIII

We have already noted that the image of the Yankee schoolmarm is necessarily revised if we consider Samuel Chapman Armstrong's Hampton teaching staff of eight northern maidens. But what of the strenuous regimen and stern taboos of Hampton's daily rounds, meant to subdue "the beast" in dark young southern men seeking instruction? From Harlan's accounts, it seems the general himself made time for framed "play." Washington's biographer writes as follows in a description that bears full quotation:

> The teachers were determined to be paragons of starched New England virtue in the sensuous South; and they were as inhibited in their social relations with the black students as the English people of Forster's *Passage to India*. . . .When General Armstrong was home, however, his strenuously active temperament occasionally found its outlet in sport. One spring evening the teacher holding study hall came in from the barracks saying: "What have you all been doing? The noise was so disturbing the girls could hardly study!" She learned that the ladies had been playing "I spy" in the yard, under the General's leadership. He also sometimes romped with the women teachers in a wild game of tag that produced fre-

> quent loud screams. If there were less innocent entertainments, they were discreetly hidden by a teacher corps devoted to setting examples for their charges. (69)

"Example," indeed. When Washington met General Armstrong, he deemed him from the outset "a perfect man: I was made to feel that there was something about him that was superhuman" (44). Here, for Booker, was the exemplary "Great Man" so rapturously praised in Thomas Carlyle's *Of Heroes and Hero Worship.*[25] Here, as well, was the black adolescent's moment of existential recognition . . . and recovery of the absent father. Harlan writes: "Not only in a Freudian but in a literal sense, General Armstrong became the illegitimate mulatto boy's father, the 'most significant other,' his paternal protector, fosterer, and guide not only during his school days but for the rest of his life. . . . Washington came to model his career, his school, his social outlook, and the very cut of his clothes after Armstrong's example" (58). If Washington secures access to the Yankee woman's purity by way of sweeping, he secures, through psychological identification with Armstrong, at least a fantasized man's privilege of play among light-complected maidens. The family romance is thus performatively completed within southern-time frames of the Freedmen's Bureau's "northern missionary" project.

However, we must consider precisely what the Family Romance is when it is not simply sitting down to properly prepared dinners at elegantly set family tables marked by civil conversation and endearing courtesies. For, of course, the "tables" at Hampton Institute were separate and quite unequal. White faculty, staff, and administration did not eat with their "colored" charges. The illegitimate mulatto's Family Romance is, then, less than inclusively civil and polite. It is, in effect, a psychodrama of fatherly annihilation—competition to the death between Great Man Father and Dark Usurping Son—vacancy and occupation as differentiated male strivings.

Given Washington's unceremonious patrimony *(partus sequitur ventrem),* he would have possessed an obsessive anxiety about Great White Men of power such as Armstrong. Compelled to come before them in public, he fears "making a fool" of himself, is ambivalent about his blunt rejection by the father, and trembles at possibilities of the return of the father's wrath as bodily harm, or, the Law (in the formulations of Jacques Lacan) as phallic economy.[26] Within southern racial economies, the aspiring mulatto's ambivalence is surely prompted by his reluctance to outdo the father at "tag," therein confirming, not the son's superhumanness but rather his bestial *black* hypersexuality.

Still, only an equitable *performance* or a clear public victory by the son can gain the mother's regard. Further intricacies are occasioned by black-South racial positionality as the "real" black mother is displaced by the bodies and morality of Mrs. Ruffner and Miss Mary Mackie.

The "matter of color" creates for black-South performance daunting frames of reference. It complicates public works and family affiliation. For, precisely what implicit ideals, standards, images must loom in the conscious and unconscious of a southern black boy who seeks to outperform the Great White Father? There can reside, of course, nothing short of a reflexive and ever doubling derealization. Or a carnivalesque "masquerade" (of which we shall have more to say later). The matter of color plays and performs in relation to two distinct southern scenes and screens.

XIV

The first screen is epidermal. On it, blackness plays the bodily drama between "I" and the violently antiblack implications of a southern white supremacist "Thou." Where the soma or body is concerned, black, public *performance anxiety* translates not as social phobia but as the specific phobia of that which exists—i.e., that screen hanging, or suspended, as Richard Wright would have it, "Between the World and Me":

> And one morning while in the woods I stumbled suddenly
> upon the thing
> Stumbled upon it in a grassy clearing guarded by scaly oaks and
> elms.

And the sooty details of the scene rose, thrusting themselves
between the world and me. . . .
There was a design of white bones slumbering forgottenly upon
a cushion of ashes.
There was a charred stump of a sapling pointing a blunt finger
accusingly at the sky.
There were torn tree limbs, tiny veins of burnt leaves, and a
scorched coil of greasy hemp;
A vacant shoe, an empty tie, a ripped shirt, a lonely hat, and a
pair of trousers stiff with black blood.

. . . .

And while I stood my mind was frozen with a cold pity for the
life that was gone.

. . . .

Now I am dry bones and my face a stony skull staring in yellow
surprise at the sun.[27]

"Derealization," dissolution of the black-South male body is the literal essence of the screen and *scene* Wright portrays in his famous meditation on lynching "Between the World and Me." The black male body is not set trembling by "fantasized" fear of psychic castration, but is set torturously quivering by what the writer Walter White called *Rope and Faggot*.[28] When one is too blackly "public," there is always danger of the white patriarch's surveillance, exclusion, lynching. This is the "strange fruit" of the southern writer Lillian Smith; it is the black "thing" rendered uncannily lyrical by the blues genius of Billie Holiday.[29] It is, alas tragically, 1998 Jasper, Texas, in the United States of America . . . the dismembered and decapitated body of James Byrd Jr.[30]

We recall the mulatto on board the train in *Up from Slavery* who causes a white conductor consternation. The conductor is unsure of the passenger's race and whether or not he should be in the car designated for blacks. The conductor, therefore, bows and surveys the man's feet. "That will settle" the matter, thinks Washington (69). And, indeed it does settle the place and placement of bodily matters. Black manhood—despite the nearly imperceptible "race" of the passenger—does not "lose one of its members." Because, even though light-complected, the Negro is, in fact, in his place in the Jim Crow car. This play on the size of the feet and the sign "member" must have equally delighted and terrified Washington's audiences—both black and white.

If the black public performance standard, conceived in terms of the soma or black body, suggests dissolution and terror, the mental screen or scene of black publicness summons anxieties of a divided consciousness. For whom—or, better, as whom?—does public blackness perform? No one captures this dilemma of the mental or *cognitive screen* suspended between the world and me better than W. E. B. Du Bois, who writes as follows in *The Souls of Black Folk:*

> After the Egyptian and Indian, the Greek and Roman, the Teuton and Mongolian, the Negro is a sort of seventh son, born with a veil, and gifted with second-sight in this American world—a world which yields him no true self-consciousness, but only lets him see himself through the revelation of the other world. It is a peculiar sensation, this double-consciousness, this sense of always looking at one's self through the eyes of others, of measuring one's soul by the tape of a world that looks on in amused contempt and pity. One ever feels his twoness, an American, a Negro; two souls, two thoughts, two unreconciled strivings; two warring ideals in one dark body, whose dogged strength alone keeps it from being torn asunder. (45)

XV

The "veil" is Du Bois's metaphor for what might be thought of as the "edge" of the performative frame, the dissonant rim where safe, colored parochialism is temptingly and provisionally refigured as anguished mulatto cosmopolitanism. The "veil" hangs in the performative moment like a scrim between dark, pastoral, problematic folk intimacy with black consciousness, and free-floating anxieties of a public mulatto modernism that subjects one to the white "gaze." The "veil" is the counterpart, in cognition or mental life, to the lynched "member" of the somatic or bodily screen. The veil hangs as maddeningly and terrifyingly as the lynched body, between the white world and public emergence of a modern *blackness*.

It is in his encounters with another of General Armstrong's teachers at Hampton Institute that Booker T. Washington discovers his personal black-South strategy for effectively negotiating both southern cognitive and bodily *screens* of color like those portrayed by Wright and Du Bois. Washington writes:

> Whatever ability I may have as a public speaker I owe in a measure to Miss [Nathalie] Lord. When she found out that I had some inclination in this direction, she gave me private lessons in the matter of breathing, emphasis, and articulation. Simply to be able to talk in public for the sake of talking has no attraction for me. In fact, I consider that there is nothing so empty and unsatisfactory as mere abstract public speaking; but from my early childhood I have had a desire to do something to make the world better, and then be able to speak to the world about that thing. (64–65)

Here, "sweeping" and purification give way to public-speaking instruction, rendered in private. Miss Lord and Washington could be seen together as he devotedly rowed her about Hampton Bay, or in their extracurricular Bible and prayer sessions, which she instituted, or during the added Sunday Christian worship she conducted in her room after official Sunday services at Hampton were adjourned. Her significance, and that of public speaking and the performance of Washington's black-South "I," are most clearly realized when Booker is invited back to Hampton after the completion of his studies to give the postgraduate address in 1879. Louis Harlan writes:

> He entitled his post-graduate address "The Force That Wins," and he and his old teacher Nathalie Lord tested and polished its phrases in an effort to out-Armstrong Armstrong. Years later she vividly remembered those rehearsals in the chapel of Virginia Hall. "I can see his manly figure, his strong, expressive face, and hear his voice so powerful and earnest when a thought required it, yet gentle and tender as he spoke of the low estate of some of

> his people." Miss Lord kept the original copy of "The Force That Wins" among her prize possessions. (99–100)

What better title for the public challenge to "out-Armstrong Armstrong" than a duly ironic "force that wins"?

The "prize possession" that Washington explicitly gained from public performance was private attentions and deep affection from the white maiden, Miss Lord. I want to suggest that the reason Booker T. Washington unfailingly grew anxious before sweeping, or speaking, or, for all we know, rowing on the bay, was because he knew both the cognitive (the veil) and somatic (lynched body) screens on which the mind of the South would read black "manly" public performances of the "force that wins."

Washington knew the implications of his purifying intimacy and instruction in "breathing lessons" among white women. After all, the ideal of his performance—the model always the object or goal of his articulate "force that wins"—was none other than the Great White Father Armstrong himself. Washington arrived at anxious cognitive and somatic realizations that a black performing "I" could strategically displace the supremacist wrath of such a father, secure access to the light-skinned woman's maiden body and affections, and, brilliantly, ameliorate cognitive dissonance by tenderly speaking of "doing things" *only* in service of one's people.

Like "sweeping" in the intimacy of the white woman's presence, Washington's public speaking is replete in its black-South performance with totem and taboo, purity and danger. His was always a black body on a very thin line between seriousness and play when he went public. What has been missed by some previous critical readings (including my own) of that "line" is, of course, the Family Romance of mulatto modernity—the dread of the white father publicly overcome by the "force that wins," orchestrated in concert with light-skinned women's abetment. Publicly, he is a lean, young mulatto, dressed in the very cut of the white father's vestments, speaking the "force" of a hidden or potential power of *blackness* (cognitive and somatic) that could win.

Could win, mind you, not an "abstract" victory as in debate. But secure fond regard from the "maidens" in the manner of Armstrong, as well as philanthropic dollars from white men happy that Washington was doing, as one donor phrased it, "our work for us" *(scopare)*.

XVI

Of course, behind the psychodrama of Washington's black male public performance and expenditure—or, better, completely imbricated with it—were the "country districts" of the South. In these districts, as in the laboring-class neighborhoods of Malden, blacks, dirt, and the "contaminations" of sexual excess and disease were rampant. The more eloquent, vivid, and effective Washington's public speaking performances on tender behalf of the black "masses" became, the more paradoxically affiliated he had to become with the "diseased family" whom he proclaimed (or declaimed) to serve. The lean, muscular, oratorically performing body of the black-South mulatto, clad in the Great White Father's clothes, is nearly hysterical with anxiety before each public occasion. Will the white audience see and hear modernity or read, in the very color and black "manliness" of his occupancy of the dais, possible contamination and failure? Washington's public-speaking mulatto body becomes metonymic of and for the framing of race, and "the race." And Tuskegee Institute itself becomes, through time and the force that wins, the purified, ideal black mother, steeped in "white" purity. For the school, Washington extended, and often overreached, himself until the moment of his death. He and his three successive New England–bred, mulatto wives serviced an institute devoted to sweeping the "county districts," instructing . . . speaking away contaminations of black libidinousness, the contagion of "sexuality" as disease. The announced project of Tuskegee Institute was to overcome the stigma of the black-South's mass body, as well as the cognitive dissonance of the veil of black soul making, in order to create bountiful black craft workers. The principal stated aim was to instill in, or against, the "country districts" a domestic "science" of hygienic black-mass life that would secure the approbation of Great White Fathers . . . and

Yankee maidens . . . especially those with philanthropic dollars to spare.

The psychological dynamics, anxieties, phobias, and panic of publicly performing such scientific magic of social change can only be understood in the context—the frame—of the mind of a virulently white supremacist South. This South did not welcome Afromodernity. And Washington did not strive publicly to press citizenship claims, voting rights, or social integration for the "country districts." Like his public address, his scientific clean-up project was a matter of anxious sweeping, mending, disinfecting, containment of "the beast."

The phrase "containment of the beast" springs directly from the missionary imperatives of Hampton Institute, where General Armstrong designed a monstrously strenuous daily schedule for his black "charges" so they would have no leftover vigor for nocturnal impropriety, sexual or otherwise.

Washington came to associate the black body's uninstructed appetites (whether for sex or for consumer goods such as sewing machines and home musical organs) with dirt. Such black appetites were, indeed, mental, material, and *corporeal* matters out of place. The "beast," then, is dangerous libidinous black bodily sexuality and desire of the "country districts." In these districts is a miasma of contaminating influences that produce blacks' urge to abandon manual labor for a smattering of learning in Latin and Greek. The "dirt" of black districts prompts black men to desert agriculture in favor of theology. It seductively urges upon even the meanest of black orators a career in politics.

The "beast" is that which distracts the black masses from a foundational, missionary cleanliness and a simplicity of agrarian purpose. Here is Washington's own foreswearing of the beast, his avowed commitment to the service of his people: "As for my individual self, it appeared to me to be reasonably certain that I could succeed in political life, but I had a feeling that it would be a rather selfish kind of success—individual success at the cost of failing to do my duty in assisting in laying a foundation for the masses."

If instinctual, or even bestial, desires to escape manual labor and the soil were "native" to the black masses of the "country districts," then Washington felt qualified to institutionalize at Tuskegee the sanitizing of such desires. He would purify black desires allied to the black libidinous body—a body screened, and held in mythic suspension, by the white mind of the South.

XVII

Though Washington clearly knows and asserts in *Up from Slavery* that the federal government—the nation at large—sacrificed the black masses during Reconstruction by its failure to establish educational, economic, and property interests for the black majority, he nevertheless refuses to critique this American failure in any robust manner. Rather, he sets himself the task and enjoins the black majority of the southern country districts to "cast down your buckets where you are." Snatch a mud-sill local success from gross national failure. If the "beastly" residue of slavery consists of millions of black Americans left penniless and "heathen" by the carnage of civil war and the ineffectualness of postwar federal administration, then there is nothing for it but to *clean them up.* Such sweeping purification is, in fact, inextricable from a marshaling of the black body to attention, discipline, regimentation, rudimentary craft, and agricultural skills like those endorsed by Tuskegee Institute. Essentially, Tuskegee becomes the black "shadow" of General Armstrong's own Hampton Institute. But missionary restraints on *blackness* are perhaps firmer at Tuskegee. In Armstrong's camp, fitting Negroes out for the "modern" meant teaching them the virtues of their own lowly estate and the abject benefits of staying tremblingly in their southern "place."

Washington, at the beginning of his Tuskegee work as he describes it in his narrative, sees the black majority as redeemable. With wistful sleight of hand, he writes: "While the coloured people [of the country districts surrounding Tuskegee] were ignorant, they had not, as a rule degraded and weakened their bodies by vices such as are common to the lower class of people in large cities" (73). When he actually tours the back country, however, Washington articulates a picture of abjection, misdirection, hygienic incompetence, corrosive diet, spendthrift ignorance, sexual explicitness, inept manners, abhorrent one-room shanties that leave him convinced: "The work to be done in order to lift these people up seemed almost beyond accomplishing" (78). What, indeed, would "modernity" consist of for such an abjectly miserable millions of black people? Here, we come to the signifying and performative "costs" of Washington's possession of "the force that wins." Indisputably, Booker T. placed himself in a position where, on a public conveyance (a railway carriage) headed South, he chivalrously and suavely took tea with two white ladies—in the very presence of white southern men who knew his work and did not have cause to examine his shoe size. It is also true, however, that Washington never moved to a position where he could relax the boundaries of his self-created, performed identity as the "son" of Armstrong. He had always to pay scrupulous attention to the line, the rim of the frame, allowing him minimal breathing room both for himself, and for "the race."

Washington's "raceless mobility" on the rails (especially if we consider the case of the train conductor already discussed . . . and, of course, *Plessy v. Ferguson*) is extraordinary in ways the narrator of *Up from Slavery* fully comprehends. However, what is never made as unequivocally clear as the facts warrant is that Booker's "peculiar mobility" is both determinately *personal* and *purchased,* at the price of a commitment to imperialism as Tuskegee Institute's normative relationship to the black "country districts." If Booker T. wishes successfully and publicly to don the weeds of Armstrong's power, sexual advantage, and missionary esteem, he must assume the role of black imperialist to the "country districts."

Hence, the education toward "modernity" that Tuskegee Institute proposes seems in perfect accord with the great Henry Adams's description of the son of Robert E. Lee, whom he met as a Harvard undergraduate. In *The Education of Henry Adams,* Adams writes: "Strictly speaking, the Southerner had no mind; he had temperament. . . . [H]e could not analyze an idea, and he could not even conceive of admitting two." As a black southerner, Booker T. Washington wants the black masses to be rid of all ideas of *education* that produce high-hatted (or swallow-tail-coated) black urban dandies infected by politics, preaching, and the fast, cosmopolitan life of modern cities.

Washington wishes to provide "educational instruction" that brings the body under control. And labor without recompense seems a fit inroad on the project of "modernity" for the black masses: "From the very beginning, at Tuskegee, I was determined to have the students do not only the agricultural and domestic work, but to have them erect their own buildings. . . . [T]he school would not only get the benefit of their labour, but the students themselves would be taught to see not only utility in labour, but beauty and dignity, would be taught, in fact, how to lift labour up from mere drudgery and toil, and would learn to love work for its own sake" (95). What this amounts to, of course, is a zealous aestheticization of slavery as "modernity."

Walter Benjamin, in seeking to define the powers of the French poet Charles Baudelaire, produces the *flâneur* as a critical category.[31] The *flâneur* is a mobile, observant, multiply personalitied city wanderer as exemplar of modernism. "Mobility" was, of course, precisely what slave law from the seventeenth-century statutes of Virginia to, I would argue, present-day southern chain gangs and America's maximum security prisons, sought to disallow for an abject southern "blackness." And what Booker T. Washington offers as performative "modernity" to the black masses is the exact *opposite* of privileges and opportunities of Benjamin's *flâneur*. In contrast to education that produces excess, luxury, urbanity, book learning, and the accessorized body, Washington urges a clean, thrifty, rural, industrial, plain style—*domesticated immobility* as the regimen for the black body of the "country districts."

XVIII

In his study of Baudelaire, Benjamin's style is evocative and laconic, not lucidly analytical. He seeks to identify the relationship of Baudelaire's life and art and the commerce and culture of France during the Second Empire. The signal manifestation of that empire, and its commerce and trade, was the emergence of the "big city" as a space of convergence for class and race, high and low cultures, technology and beaux arts, new building materials and fecund ideologies of the state, bleak factories and tawdry parks for the working class, popular dioramas and precious lyric poetry, military conflict at urban barricades and demolition of "antiquity" to facilitate urban "airiness" and army mobilization. The role enacted by Baudelaire to negotiate this urban mélange was *flâneur*.

The *flâneur* strolls in Parisian arcades (covered spaces of new department stores and textile merchants). For the *flâneur*, the *crowd* offers an indicative spectacle of "modernism." Whether in parks designed for the populace at large, or in arcades constructed of iron and its decor, the *flâneur* is

> [not] the pedestrian who would let himself be jostled by the crowd, but . . . [one] who demanded elbow room and was unwilling to forego the life of a gentleman of leisure. Let the many attend to their daily affairs; the man of leisure can indulge in the perambulations of the *flâneur* only if as such he is already *out of place*. He is as much out of place in an atmosphere of complete leisure as in the feverish turmoil of the city. (129; my emphasis)

I take these words of Benjamin as a summation of the *flâneur* and his evolution. The history commences with Bohemia, among "conspiratorial" and potentially revolutionary cadres of the city. It traces a metamorphosis into the "poet who roams the city in search of rhyme-booty . . . [displaying the jerky gait and collection tendencies for refuse of the ragpicker]." The evolution terminates in the figure of the "dandy" (96). Modernism and "high capital," Benjamin suggests, are inseparable from a peculiar brand of both architecture and heroism that look to urban masses as inspiration, spectacle, exemplars of the future, nemesis. In his evolutionary—or, *entropic, catabolic, suicidal*—history, the *flâneur* is inseparable from evolving forms of modern markets, arts, journalism, popular entertainments, technological and architectural innovation. Everything conduces toward the *flâneur*'s locative instability. He is forever *out of place*. His rich personification and urban (re)development find counterpart in men's fashion. Whose "weeds" one wears (the manner in which one "interprets" and "mobilizes" them) signal the modern order one endorses.

IXX

Alas, the "modern" black body, for the black masses Washington patronizes, is the body aware of virtues of the toothbrush, content with meager rewards of Tuskegee's ill-equipped instruction and industrial trades. Washington, finally, defines only his *own* success at *personal mobility in disguise.* By the phrase, I intend a comprador's wardrobe, replete with the jazziness of racial cross-dressing, homoerotic display and liaisons dangerous among white rough riders like President Roosevelt, and "power ties" after the manner of Armstrong. Washington writes as follows:

> After considerable experience in coming into contact with wealthy and noted men, I have observed that those who have accomplished the greatest results are those who "keep under the body"; are those who never grow excited or lose self-control, but are always calm, self-possessed, patient, and polite. I think that President William McKinley is the best example of a man of this class that I have ever seen. (126)

Surely, Washington's encomium to President McKinley coincides with W. J. Cash's observations on the courtier-like appeal of the southern planter class.

What is missing from Booker T.'s paean to McKinley is the global, political imperialist "work" accomplished by a president who kept "under the body." McKinley's administration purchased the Philippines, annexed Hawaii, acquired Puerto Rico and Guam as protectorates of the United States—and pushed through the "open door" policy that allowed commercial, imperialist access to China. This president of the United States seems to have been far more adept at keeping bodies of the "other" abject and *under* than with any program equivalent to a New Age somatics of temperance and tranquility.

I want to suggest that at the moment Washington achieved his most exalted performative competence at the "force that wins," both he and the black-South mass body were inert with respect to public mobility, cosmopolitanism, an effectual Afro-modernity.

A *mobility of the black flâneur* . . . to be purposefully fantastic . . . such movement would have brought the black majority not "under the body" of white law, but into the national public sphere with citizenship rights, critical intellectual skills par excellence, technological abilities suited to opportunities of "Progress" . . . in the northern sense of that term. Washington settled instead for a personal triumphalism and an imperialist power over the back country that were, indeed, remarkable for a black man of his day, but far from the *black fantastic,* then or now. Washington was an imperialist educator without peer . . . among the "country districts."

The significance of education for the culture of dominance, of course, is that it enforces and surveils mind and manners in the service of the "public good." Education becomes the *mission civilatrice* for colonialism everywhere. Consider Indian boarding schools in the United States. Such schools were designed precisely to eradicate the "Indian" in a Native American self, and self-consciousness. Indian schools changed the names, dress, hair, and minds of Native Americans forced into them by ruthless Christian zeal.

The connection between both Washington and his mentor Armstrong can be seen, of course, in their relationship precisely to Indian "education." Washington is chosen by Armstrong to oversee the eradication of "Indianness" from those "captives" whom Armstrong "experimentally" admits to Hampton. Though Washington claims to have made "progress" with his Indian students, he seems quite uncharacteristically ironic about the implications of his civilizing pedagogy, concluding that "no white American ever thinks that any other race is wholly civilized until he wears the white man's clothes, eats the white man's food, speaks the white man's language, and professes the white man's religion" (67). However, Washington foreshadows his own complicity with such a "white man's view" when he writes of his first full-time teaching job in Malden as follows: "In addition to the usual routine of teaching, I taught the [black] pupils to comb their hair, and to keep their hands and faces clean, as well as their clothing.

I gave special attention to teaching them the proper use of the tooth-brush and the bath. In all my teaching I have watched carefully the influence of the tooth-brush, and I am convinced that there are few single agencies of civilization that are more far-reaching" (69).

After one has been "educated"—stripped of past habits, language, and modes of being—and "incorporated," not *into* the body public but *as* the assimilated, marginal, darkly in-place *shadow of civilization,* one's consciousness will surely be whiter/yea whiter than snow. Manners, performance, psychology, education conspire to produce disciplined "colonized purity."

XX

The title bestowed on Washington and his institution by his best biographer is "Master of the Tuskegee Plantation." Yes, Washington, literally and publicly, worked within the framing mind of the South to produce not a utopia of black modernism at Tuskegee, but a retrograde and imperialist plantation. This plantation was brokerage ground for Booker T.'s own *personal* power, wealth, and influence over national "Negro affairs." In truth, after achieving the "intimacy" of the "force that wins" as public performance, Washington's program never broke the frame. All subsequent new and anxious public performances merely affirmed the "rightness" of the Old and New South's claims for regional, philosophical *difference* from a dandified, industrial North. Washington fashioned himself as one of white America's best champions of infinite *deferral* ("all deliberate speed") of black citizenship and southern public sphere rights for the black masses.

When, in the early twentieth century, Rabbi Charles Fleischer attempted to compare Washington's views of black American accommodationism to what the rabbi considered an effective strategy for American Jews, the rabbi failed to reckon that he was addressing a black Boston Literary and Historical Association keenly aware of Tuskegee's imperialist suppression of mobile, black modernity. Washington's biographer notes that at the rabbi's mere mention of the principal's name, "a frost fell upon the audience that had been warmly sympathetic" (35). Harlan continues: "Fleischer and many others failed to understand how Washington's role as interracial diplomat was based on ambiguity, how Washington had license to criticize but not challenge the white supremacy system, since his own position of preeminence rested on his accommodation to the system" (35). What Washington's program sacrificed of essential *mobility* for black America was occasioned (and surely the black Boston audience knew this) by Euroamerican ideas and forces that were equally crippling *for both blacks and Jews* in their relationship to modernity.

And here the discussion reflexively, comparatively, and methodologically doubles back upon itself.

For there is, of course, a perfect psychoanalytical segue to be provoked between the rabbi's advocacy of Washingtonianism and the nineteenth-century labors of Sigmund Freud. In Vienna, most anti-Semitic of all European cities (not unlike a framing white-supremacist mind of the South with respect to blackness), Freud's necessities with respect to the Jewish body or soma were not color but *lack*. Sander Gilman engagingly demonstrates in his astute scholarly work that the objective correlative of the Jewish *lack* conditioning Freud's performance was the circumcised penis of the Jewish male body.[32] Gilman has done heroic work analyzing Freud's confrontation with the dilemma of a "country district" of Jewish difference. And, Gilman avers, Freud wrote off critical Jewish male *lack* as the deficiency and "hysteria" of *Woman*.

Washington scapegoats and imperializes the black masses in order to wear the master's weeds; Freud, in Gilman's view, sacrifices *Woman* to construct his own personal psychoanalytic authority as a flawless public speaker of German . . . an achieved practitioner of *science*. (A "science" closer to Rampersad's provocative injunctions than to a rigorous Newtonian empiricism.)

Freud's "analytics," then, are as much a discourse of accommodationist "modernism" as Booker T. Washington's. Obviously, the ambivalence and scapegoating of Freud in the office of *science* go some way toward addressing Rampersad's query about black intellectuals' reservations before psychoanalytical criticism . . . or psychobiography, Freudian style. Perhaps, only a deliberately "fantastic" postmodernism breaks frames. But, as surely as the processes of Lacanian signification maintain the rule that "the signifier is the subject for another signifier,"[33] we know that public speaking *cannot* lead to public sphere mobility if the speaker hears only his fantasized master's voice—is wedded, that is, exclusively to the "Names of the Fathers."

XXI

There is a certain psychosis in the transformation of black abjection to black public-sphere mobility. We have yet to understand it. (In the recent black film *Juice,* the character Bishop, played by the late Tupac Shakur, knows that black men in particular have to be "crazy" in order to survive postindustrial America. That Ernest Dickerson's independent effort displaces psychosis with a black, male rap DJ—played by Omar Epps—bringing orderly "noise" is disabling to the film's *force.* However, the fact that a brilliantly talented Shakur is now "the late" indicates either that Tupac was not "crazy" enough . . . or, that we, who live after him, are hopelessly belated.) There are carnivalesque ironies of imposture, disguise, and mobility, then, to which we must turn in the service of a new American scholarship. Specifically, I believe white studies has convincingly put before us analyses that enlarge our prospect on the public work of both Booker T. Washington and "public" American blackness in general.

For, at the very moment when Booker T. was seeking to create a modern, pastoral, black labor force from the reserves of the "country districts," Irish workers and other white immigrants in the North were exalting in blackface minstrelsy. This exaltation and performance, according to Eric Lott and David Roediger, entailed immigrants' assumption of *blackface performance*, spectacle, and masquerade as signifying practices that nostalgically dignified "foundational" values of a pastoral lifestyle that was fast disappearing under the pressures of nineteenth-century American industrialization.[34] Describing the work of historian George Rawick in his own book titled *The Wages of Whiteness,* Roediger notes: "All of the old habits [sexual promiscuity, quickness to action, agrarianism, immediate gratification of the senses] so recently discarded by whites adopting capitalist values came to be fastened onto Blacks" (95).

Minstrelsy, therefore, as trafficked by immigrant and white working-class cohorts from the mid- to the late-nineteenth century, represents a mirror image of Washington's framed assumption of General Armstrong's white "force." Minstrelsy is racial theft; it wears a peculiarly nineteenth-century southern American cast. Eric Lott writes as follows in *Love and Theft: Blackface Minstrelsy and the American Working Class:*

> [White] minstrel performers often attempted to repress through ridicule the real interest in black cultural practices they nonetheless betrayed—minstrelsy's mixed erotic economy of celebration and exploitation . . . [comprises both] "love and theft," the very form of blackface acts—an investiture in black bodies—seems a manifestation of the particular desire to try on the accents of "blackness" and demonstrates the permeability of the color line. . . . It was cross-racial desire that coupled a nearly insupportable fascination and self-protective derision with respect to black people and their cultural practices, and that made blackface minstrelsy less a sign of absolute white power and control than of panic, anxiety, terror, and pleasure. (6)

Minstrelsy is thus coded as white *performance anxiety* . . . moving directionally from white to black in nineteenth-century America. And we scarcely need *DSM-IV* to tell us which way such racialized winds did blow, whose sails they benefited.

Lott goes on, astutely, to analyze ways in which white working popular discourse *(framing?)* of *blackness* both soothed white fears and "became a metonym for class" (72). Through racialized blackface, a white American artisanate became a white "class." Roediger notes the context in which *race* and *class* formation in the United States are co-implicated, and perhaps coterminous: "Both white slavery metaphors and working class abolitionism served to locate the position of hired labor within a *slaveholding* republic. Both failed because they could not do so unproblematically. Comparisons of white workers with slaves, which are too often considered as simply *class* expressions, were shot through with resonances regarding America's racial realities" (86). Panic, terror, anxiety, pleasure, love, theft, race, class, ridicule, attraction—these words orbit a general economy of minstrelsy's white *performance anxiety* like allegorical phantasmagoria. They all collapse though into the signal category of *masquerade*—to which, much earlier, I promised to return.

XXII

It seems to me that both Lott and Roediger—and the most canny labor histories—urge the utter indivisibility of race and class as sites of *masquerade* in the definition of *work* and working men's identities in America. Roediger writes: "Blackface performances tended to support pro-slavery and white supremacist politics" (124). In the same ways, presumably, that Irish working-class mobs, chanting for blacks to be sent "back to Africa," abetted labor relations and dynamics of southern slavery. Roediger argues in fact that minstrelsy's *masquerade* was the most effective white cultural mobilizer of all: "Minstrelsy made a contribution to a sense of popular whiteness among workers across lines of ethnicity, religion, and skill. It achieved a common symbolic language—a unity—that could not be realized by racist crowds, by political parties or by labor unions. Blackface whiteness [masquerade] meant respectable rowdiness and safe rebellion" (127). In Lacanian terms, minstrelsy is the "symbolic order" of both *class* and *race* formation in the United States.[35]

What, then, of a Booker T. Washington, who hugged to himself strategies of topsy-turvydom and transgressive performance that stood minstrelsy on its head? What of Washington's personal white masquerade?

Roediger notes that: "Irish-Americans . . . treasured their whiteness as entitling them to both political rights and to jobs" (136). Their "sampling blackness" (my own phrase, drawn from technologies of present-day rap music) was both an empowering and mass-mobilizing strategy. By contrast, Washington's masquerade, insofar as it was not an overt pedagogy or an open curriculum of Tuskegee Institute, represented preeminently the black principal's *personal triumph in white drag.* It is Lott who most persuasively records the radical potential of immigrant, blackface minstrelsy's masquerade:

> [White] minstrel performers gave [the Bohemian] pattern an American spin. Most of them were minor, apolitical theatrical men of the northern artisanate who pursued a newly available bourgeois dream of freedom and play by paradoxically coding themselves as "black." Marginalized by temperament, by habit (often alcoholism), by ethnicity, even by sexual orientation, these artists immersed themselves in blackness . . . that imaginary space of fun and license outside (but structured by) Victorian bourgeois norms. (51)

Had Washington dedicated himself to black *mass-mobilization toward citizenship,* and taught the black majority of the country districts how to "dress for success," southern black America might well have been on its way to an empowering modernity, well in advance of *Brown v. Board of Education.* Having arrived at such a desirous "if" with respect to one aspect of the founding black leader/father, I can now provide the following provisional work-up of those ever demanding tight places of black being in the Americas:

TIGHT PLACES: *the psycho-social figurations of the sexually forbidden, whether the white (maiden?) woman in southern planter class economies of honor and desire, or, the black male body in disciplined or incarcerated "posture of appeal" before a strong white arm's lordship and allure. In sum, the always ambivalent cultural compromises of occupancy and vacancy, differentially effected by contexts of situations: that is, Who moves? Who doesn't?*

XXIII

Modernism's emphasis falls on the locative—where one is located or placed—in determining how constricted the domain of freedom might be. But to be socially located is, of course, to be already divided. The weaning from the mother's breast; witnessing of the primal scene in which both mother and father have the "penis"; incumbencies of the symbolic order of language, replete with all those (to invoke Lacan) "symbolic fathers" who take the mother away . . . herein lies the creation of the social "subject."[36] This subject is created, as post-Freudian psychologists tell us, in *difference predicated on lack*. Who has and who does not have . . . the penis . . . but no, not so much that physical biological appendage, but instead, who is most adept at sustaining *the symbolic, representational illusions and delusions the mere appendage generates*? Symbolic differentiation moves along axes of *power*.

This post-Freudian psychoanalytic account of differentiation's *power* translates—at least with respect to Booker T. Washington's *Up from Slavery*—as an implicit, inescapable plane of *gender signification* throughout the narrative. Washington's donning the weeds of Armstrong is a treacherous act. It is an act of symbolic murder . . . of the white father . . . who absented/secreted himself in the primal scene with Booker T.'s mother. To take on the white father's clothes and "play" like a white man is, for Booker T. Washington, to negotiate a familiar—indeed, "tight-spaced"—drama of sexual role-play within the framing mind of the South.

A now classic site for reading such gender masquerade as Washington's interracial cross dressing is Joan Riviere's essay "Womanliness as a Masquerade," published in 1929 in the *International Journal of Psychoanalysis*.[37] (It was the inimitable historian Joan Scott who directed me to Riviere's work. Much like the undergraduate who did not have the "blues," I did not have the signifying gender psychoanalytics I needed fully to see Washington's sweep.) Riviere writes of one of her analysands:

> The exhibition in public of her intellectual proficiency, which was in itself carried through successfully, signified an exhibition of herself in possession of the father's penis, having castrated him. This display once over, she was seized by horrible dread of the retribution the father would then exact. Obviously it was a step towards

> propitiating the avenger to endeavor to offer herself to him sexually. (37)

(Here, in woman's weeds, is Booker T.'s "performance anxiety" with a vengeance!) Describing yet another analysand—a quite brilliant scholar in her intellectual field of endeavor—Riviere writes:

> When lecturing, not to students but to colleagues, she chooses particularly feminine clothes. Her behavior on these occasions is also marked by an inappropriate feature: she becomes flippant and joking, so much so that it has created comment and rebuke. She has to treat the situation of displaying her masculinity to men as a "game," as something *not real,* as a "joke." She cannot treat herself as on equal terms with men; moreover, the flippant attitude enables some of her sadism to escape, hence the offence it causes. (39)

Riviere's project is analytically to distinguish conditions that make for "real" womanliness—"womanliness" that bears no pathological or dissimulated trace of heterosexuality. However, the further she pursues her observations, bringing to the fore the psychological literature of her era, the more she becomes convinced (and convincing to us as readers) that there is *no* difference between the *masquerade* of "womanliness" and "woman."

To extrapolate from Riviere's analytics is to cast an entirely more intense light upon the *tightness* of place. Everything, one might say, hinges for Riviere on the identity of "true woman" and the normativity of "adornment" *as* woman. In *The Gay Science,* Nietzsche cryptically anticipates Riviere when he enjoins: "Woman is so artistic." Critiquing and elaborating Riviere's essay, the scholar Stephen Heath writes: "The masquerade serves to show what she ['woman'] does not have, a penis, by showing—the adornment, the putting-on—something else. . . . Adornment is the woman, she exists veiled; only thus can she represent lack, be what is wanted: lack 'is never presented other than as a reflection on a veil.'"[38]

Now, we have already noted the "screens" or "veils" Washington had to negotiate. In a type of nonspecific transfer for our discussion, we can assert that the *lack* of personhood (in the case of the black male, the *lack* of connection or suture between a mystical and mystified black *penis* and a white-powered *Phallus*) is the very "veiled" condition of white American personhood in general.

This, I think, is the canny truth of Roediger's and Lott's analyses of minstrelsy's masquerade. Certainly, this *lack* is the screen for white supremacy within the framing mind of the South. It prompts the scene and screen, always, of the castrating, somatic rituals of lynching.

Hence, the "posture of appeal" of Washington's manly *tight places* takes on, paradoxically, the character of a distinct black male coquettishness. Sartorial adornment is underlain by sadomasochistic fantasies; terror reads out as sleeping with the enemy . . . or *being slept with* as the "privileged" act of the enemy. (We return here, of course, to *partus sequitur ventrem.*)

Recurring to the nineteenth-century slave narrative of Frederick Douglass and to a novel by William Faulkner, we might say it is *not* incidental that Douglass's homoerotic wrestling match on a sacred Sunday with the slavebreaker Mr. Covey mirrors, in its spectatorial violent grappling, Thomas Sutpen's nocturnal couplings with his own dreamlike one hundred "wild niggers."[39] (The white daughter of Faulkner's novel is in the loft, with her black woman companion, peering, gazing at these black and white "men" masquerading in muscular intimacy.)

Shall we say then that one must make a "show" in order to identify as "subject"? The scholar Stephen Heath postulates cinema as the screen for such a show. He invokes cinema, in fact, as the special *scene* of woman's adornment, as well as the public scene of the fantastic male gaze.

This is not, one thinks, unlike the minstrel show or Booker T.'s public speaking. The Big Screen, we might infer, is the *thing* in which white, male personhood derives "consciousness" of its own social being-in-the-world . . . and of its *power.*

It is perhaps too abruptly said here, but I believe it is now entirely inferable that the performance anxieties of Booker T. Washington—his force that wins and weeds à la Armstrong—all lead along a trajectory of dread and anxiety directly to D. W. Griffith's *The Birth of a*

Nation. Griffith's founding film is white history's stalker with a knife, a visual phantasmagoria of national white manhood's feverish gaze of subject formation.

TIGHT PLACES: *Locative adornment that confirms dynamics of domination and subjugation; the artistry of castration anxieties; the jocular "dumbing down," or "sexing up" that calms or confirms the masters; the always already incumbencies of signification: that is, "sexual ambiguity" as the instrumentally necessary and sufficient condition of* power.

XXIV

Am I saying there existed a deeply homoerotic bond between Booker T. Washington and *all* white men—but in particular and most expressly between the Wizard of Tuskegee and General Armstrong? Yes. It was not *ab nihilo* that the eminent white sociologist Robert Park proclaimed the Negro as the "Lady of the races." Park (who first got on his feet in the employ of Washington and Tuskegee) articulated white male fantasy. And such fantasy gained credence and affect in "play," "on the screen" of Washingtonian public speaking.

A final note on gender carries us back to modernity as the archive of the *flâneur.* Here is Booker T. Washington on the notion of the "educated black man":

> The white people who questioned the wisdom of starting this new school [Tuskegee] had in their minds pictures of what was called an educated Negro, with a high hat, imitation gold eye-glasses, a showy walking-stick, kid gloves, fancy boots, and what not—in a word, a man who was determined to live by his wits. It was difficult for these people to see how education would produce any other kind of coloured man. (92)

The scholar Rhonda K. Garelick's intriguing study *Rising Star: Dandyism, Gender, and Performance in the Fin de Siècle* is helpful in explicating this "false ideal" of "Negro education" Washington describes.[40]

The *flâneur* or *dandy,* according to Professor Garelick, is not merely an aloof, voyeuristic, traveling, ambiguous practitioner of life as art. He is also one who ironically seeks celebrity in singularity and social success though his castigating wit. He cunningly seeks ascetic solitude in parlous, teeming parlors of the rich and famous.

Turning himself into a mystified and aesthetic *art life,* the dandy is putatively nonreproducible. But, in order to be acknowledged as successful *dandy*— exemplar of anticommercialism and *outré* taste— the dandy must be *seen* and acknowledged. Hence, he becomes that most dreaded of all things: a completely reproducible "role model" . . . and for mass culture no less. His is a commercializable masquerade. Not only do dandies multiply like preening rabbits, they become indistinguishable, in their own self-fashioned art life, from characters in art. Garelick writes:

> Dandyism . . . conflates textual and human seduction . . . [It] does not just merge the real and fictional; it creates a contagion of style and seduction. Texts about dandies strive for dandyist appeal; critics writing about dandies or their texts fall easily into dandyist style and succumb to its charms. This is, of course, how all celebrity works; and dandies are among the earliest celebrities. One cannot declare oneself a celebrity any more than one can simply state that one is charming and influential. Celebrity and influence require a vast system of communication, a network of opinion and desire. (11)

Garelick persuasively argues that the dandy's *theatricality of indifference to public opinion,* sexual ambiguity, outrageous magnificence as *poseur* lead but to the public, music hall, fin-de-siècle, theatrical "woman": Jenny Linn, Ellen Terry, Loie Fuller. In Loie Fuller's brand of cabaret theater, the elaborate, mechanistic, private performance of the dandy explodes into the age of technology. "The dandy and the woman onstage merge" (10).

Recurring to Heath, we might add that they "merge" in cinematic and distinctively racially coded American ways in the person of Al Jolson's *Jazz Singer* a few years down the line from Fuller.

My claim with respect to Booker T. Washington and *Up from Slavery*'s relationship to gender and performance is that an outrageous, terrifying, white network of power, opinion, and desire constituted Washington as *the black dandy* (kid-gloved ghost of the "educated black man" in the white imaginary) . . . all dressed up without any fully modern, urban place to go.

Ah, but as "celebrity!" he performed in public ceaselessly and got "paid in full." Washington's fin-de-siècle act was compensated, though more under terms of the "woman onstage" than it was recompensed for a multiply mutable, black modern public-sphere *flâneurship:* a black agency akin to Benjamin's Baudelairean exemplar of the future.

TIGHT PLACE: *the suit, and stage of the white general's publicly financed spectacles of His own, and owned, network of opinion and desires; scene of the "black public leader" as woman onstage.*

Coda

Despite his best efforts to keep "under the body," to revise preemptively the black body's placement before Great White Fathers and Northern Maidens, Washington's death was haunted by rumor. At St. Luke's Hospital in Manhattan, where he was admitted during the fall of 1915, the white attending physician, Dr. Bastedo, reported not only a "noticeable hardening of the arteries" but also: "Racial characteristics are, I think, in part responsible for Dr. Washington's breakdown."[41] Washington's longtime personal physician Dr. George C. Hall was outraged. In his opinion Bastedo's "racial characteristics" diagnosis signified that: "a colored man [as patient, has] 'a syphilitic history.' " Washington's biographer is superbly cautious, concluding that even if Washington was examined by a specialist in gonococcus infections during his final illness, there is *no clear evidence* that syphilis was the cause of his death.

What is significant for the present discussion, however, is the fact that the marking of the black body that constitutes America's derogation of *color* has frequently been elaborated, as we have already demonstrated, in terms of the libidinal—the black body as intemperately sexual and thus open to sexual disease and contamination, in a word, *syphilis.* (The "science" of Freud's era similarly marked the Jewish body as sexual, vulnerable to syphilitic infection: "racial characteristics.") Washington's public ritual purifications could not protect him, even in death, from "scientific" markings of his black body under the sign "syphilis." The repressed returns; it can not be swept or spoken permanently away. Tuskegee's Black Father becomes horrifying contagion. The "Mother Institute" is itself paradoxically infectious with respect to the "country districts." Like rumor, contagion spreads. I refer, of course, to the infamous Tuskegee experiment inaugurated during the 1930s by the United States Public Health Service in full cooperation with Tuskegee Institute.[42]

The Tuskegee study, which continued until it was journalistically exposed during the 1970s, was designed to observe the effects of untreated syphilis on black male bodies. Tuskegee Institute becomes, then—for almost half a century—a place of black "round-ups" in which black male victims of "modern medicine" are maliciously left in the dark about the deathly inhumanity of racialized American "science." Hundreds perished in the Tuskegee experiment, which has been compared to bizarre proceedings of Nazi doctors during the Jewish Holocaust.

Washington's token modernism entailed personal aggrandizement and, perhaps, even limited profitable southern outreach to a handful of the black masses. But the soul of the Tuskegeean's performance was compromised from the outset. He acted in the frame of a southern mind whose founding tenets he failed publicly to challenge. In the light of such failure, "public health" came to mean the same for blacks and whites, a deathly entailing of the black male body in the spectacular: in a cruel disciplinary "scientific show" of white male, shall we say, *penality*. The black-South body, on the line in public spaces must, ideally, crack a traditional frame. Contagion is only avoidable when it is *spoken against* . . . in the now . . . against the day. Nothing is more threatening to the southern *real* than the critical, informed, articulate, healthy black-mass body, *en propre personne*.

In my own "Lew-vull" southern household, Houston Sr. not only installed a "high-fidelity, stereophonic system" that must have set him back more than a few dollars but also secured the discounted black-and-white, seventeen-incher to which I have already alluded. We sat to Sunday dinner with "good music" playing—whether the Mormon Tabernacle Choir doing *The Messiah* or "Greatest Sonatas" of Beethoven. We were practically required to watch *Omnibus* (the "old school" version of *On the Road,* the Discovery Channel, and National Public Television's bill of fare). And it was on *Omnibus* that I was first mesmerized by performances of *Our Town* and other miracles of American high culture. We were taken to performances, when available, of Carol Brice at Memorial Auditorium, or Todd Duncan turning out lyrics of *Lost in the Stars.* We were given a dime for every book we read . . . boosted to a quarter if we submitted a book report. There was no question whether we would go to college and become "cultured professionals"; our options had to do only with which black college or university we would attend. Houston Sr. was keen on two historically black colleges and universities (I think because of their devotion to what Du Bois called the "university ideal" of "culture"): Howard and Fisk. So I did not leave home without it: *culture* . . . and the literate, informed idealism my father believed it fostered. All this and Cincinnati too!

Yet, as the powerful *Baltimore and Ohio* locomotive sped over the Ohio River in 1961, carrying me toward Washington, D.C., little did I realize the locale of black modernity had shifted. I was headed north, expecting to fulfill a dream of cultured modernism at Howard University. Meanwhile, in the black southern "country districts" there had commenced an articulate, body-on-the-line, frame-breaking march toward Afro-modernity. A revolutionary revision of the southern public sphere, roiling old ghosts violently up, putting cherished white-South shibboleths under black mass interrogation, was under way.

With the great southern civil rights "parting of the waters" of the 1950s and 1960s, one after another of those "tight places" conditioning the souls of black folk gave way to brilliant expressivity, canny improvisation, striking innovations, black mobility of body and mind, and, arguably, a cosmopolitan and liberatory *cultural* discourse that would have captivated even Baudelaire's *flâneur.* Especially had he encountered this discourse "under the black-mass voice" of Dr. Martin Luther King Jr. Dr. King, it now seems to me, gave to blacks and to Afro-modernity the southern "gateway" we have yet fully to analyze or comprehend. I know King's was a strategic "technology for liberation" that has, in the fullness of time, led me back home: I *am,* perhaps now really only analytically, and for the first time, in the South, and the South is hauntingly in me.

A Concluding Meditation on Plantations, Ships, and Black Modernism

Any personal autonomy allowed to—or won—by the slaves was restricted by the ferocious labour demands of the plantation, by detailed rules of conduct and by the ever-present fear of savage sanctions in the case of any real or imagined transgression. Offenders would be mercilessly flogged and deprived of all petty privileges of extra rations. Slaves could not set foot outside the plantation without express permission; however, some of the slave "elite" might regularly be able to obtain chits permitting them to go to neighbouring plantations of the local township to visit relatives or to buy or sell provisions.

ROBIN BLACKBURN, *The Making of New World Slavery*

After its brief inaugural residence in a black church, Tuskegee Institute was moved out of town. It was situated by Booker T. Washington on a few acres of land belonging to an abandoned plantation. Through ingenious credit negotiations and humble good-faith arrangements with white merchants and men of Alabama distinction, Washington made his educational enterprise viable during the early 1880s in what he describes as a "stable and a hen house." The atmospherics and regimen of Tuskegee Institute are well reflected by the school's placement. Tuskegee was a manifestly agrarian institute emphasizing labor of the soil, handicrafts, strict daily timetables borrowed from the format of General Armstrong's Hampton Institute. Significantly, the plantation chosen by Washington for occupancy was land abandoned by whites in favor of more profitable southern business enterprises such as lumbering. Roy Varner was the town white merchant who provided both land and supplies for what might be considered Washington's "retrofitting" of black American life in the New South.

For surely, to take on "abandoned lands" at the turn of the nineteenth century was to harken back, through dark and tumultuous years of Reconstruction and Redemption, to the agency so ineffectively designed after the Civil War to help blacks move up from slavery—namely, the Bureau of Refugees, Freedmen, and Abandoned Lands, colloquially known as the "Freedmen's Bureau." "Refugees" were the poorest class of whites displaced by the war; "abandoned lands" were the former estates and properties of those whites who took readily to the cause of the Confederacy. Promises were everywhere abroad by war's end, as I noted earlier, that freed blacks would be provided economic support by the Freedmen's Bureau in the form of "forty acres and a mule." Such provisions never became reality.

"Abandoned lands" were quite soon reclaimed, in fact, by treasonous "generals," "colonels," and "captains" of the Confederate Southern Army. Such men were almost immediately after the war granted pardons by President Andrew Johnson. What transpired on land reclaimed by treasonous white southern patriarchs and "officers" was a scandal of legalized black-labor exploitation—a brutalization of the black-South body that endured well into the twentieth century.

In *The Betrayal of the Negro,* the historian Rayford Logan notes that "the economic basis of second-class citizenship for Negroes was rooted deeply in slavery. On the eve of the Civil War almost nine out of ten Negroes were slaves. The vast majority of these 3,953,760 slaves were field hands and domestic servants. . . . [A]t the end of the war most Southern Negroes were without capital, without the rudiments of education and without experience in work except as agricultural field hands and as domestic servants."[1]

Citing statistics from the census reports for 1890 and 1900, Logan reveals that the economic and occupational status of the black majority—over 90 percent of whom resided in the South at the century's turn—had scarcely altered: "The failure of the tremendous expansion of American industry to change materially the essentially peasant and domestic status of most Negroes is evident from the fact that in 1890, 88% and in 1900, 86.7% of all Negroes were still employed in these least remunerative and least dignified occupations" (155). Taking into account the abject, brutal, stultifying relationship (slavery, peonage, sharecropping, convict lease labor) of black-majority *plantation arrangements* of southern life, it seems a terrible augury against black modernism that Booker T. Washington chose an "abandoned" white plantation landscape as the site for his Tuskegee uplift project.

And Washington did not simply situate his black educational enterprise physically on a *plantation*. He also instituted and argued for an essentially black peasant southern plantation economics, manners, handicrafts, and habits of mind for the black majority—life arrangements or a *habitus* that had been hallmarks of plantation black abjection under southern slavery, and indeed throughout the Americas.

Like the most enlightened white southern paternalistic despots and agrarian lords, Washington believed his own plantation project was a "mission from God" (or from white American captains of industry), ordaining him to hold "under" the black-South body. Tuskegee Institute, therefore, was only paradoxically "ahead of its time." For Washington's school was shaped and hallowed as a virtual "zone of confinement"—a redacted *plantation,* as it were, forestalling rather than fostering mobility of the black-South body beyond or out of abjection. In *Origins of the New South, 1877–1913,* C. Vann Woodward writes:

> The shortcomings of [Washington's project for the Negro] whether in education, labor, or business, were the shortcomings of a philosophy that dealt with the present in terms of the past. . . . [His] training school, and the many schools he inspired, taught crafts and attitudes more congenial to the pre–machine age than to the twentieth century. . . . [H]is labor doctrine was a compound of individualism, paternalism, and antiunionism in an age of col-

> lective labor action . . . [and] his business philosophy . . . [was] an anachronism.[2]

Tuskegee's anachronisms also included, of course, Washington's philosophy of the black majority's fit relationship to public-sphere mobility, civil society, and citizenship rights. Not only did Tuskegee's founder seem resolutely to strive to contain the "beast" and constrain the black "country districts," he also seems to have labored mightily to keep *blackness* of the "peasant" sort out of the "public eye," polling places, and urban sites of assembly. Tuskegee Institute engaged no advocacy for black majority "rights of in-town assembly."

Robert J. Norrell writes of the relationship between Tuskegee's black plantation and the adjacent white-controlled town as follows:

> [P]eaceful relations probably owed less to the happy social interaction of . . . black and white elites than to a careful effort to keep the Institute community insulated. School administrators discouraged students from going downtown, and at times prohibited them from doing so. If a student complained about being demeaned at the segregated theater, he was reminded that the Institute sponsored a movie each Saturday. The administration emphasized to students that the Institute community was a self-sufficient entity—down to having its own water and electrical supply.[3]

On the Tuskegee plantation, Washington was, in the estimate of Vann Woodward, not only confining the black "country districts" from town life and modern public-sphere possibilities, but also costuming them in outmoded fashions of the founder's youth: "Brickmaking, blacksmithing, wheelwrighting, harness making, basketry, tin-smithing—the type of crafts taught at Tuskegee—had more relevance to the South of Booker Washington's boyhood than to the [New] South of United States Steel" (365). Washington's *retrofitting* of the black majority in anachronistic vestments of peasant servility and abjection (while everywhere publicly and performatively masquerading himself seductively before "great" white men and women north and south) is surely what compelled W. E. B. Du Bois to pen his devastating critique of the founder's leadership titled "Of Mr. Booker T. Washington and Others." With stunning wit, sarcasm, and irony, Du Bois records the "narrowness" of Washington's leadership ideals, as well as the tangible retrogression (the "descent," as it were, to more abject depths than slavery) of the black "country districts" under the banners of Tuskegee Institute.

The move out of town (even beyond the solace and immunities of the autonomous black-South church) and *back* to the plantation reveals, in a sense that I shall shortly make clear, Tuskegee Institute as a perfect *disciplinary* project of its southern time and place. Tuskegee's relocation, in fact, brings once again to the fore my earlier reference to our United States', turn-of-the-millennium prison-industrial complex. We turn again, as well, to considerations of occupancy and vacancy: black public-sphere mobility and citizenship rights of assembly crucial to black modernism in the Americas.

II

I have elaborated elsewhere[4] my definition of black modernism in the United States, and surely it is apparent in my foregoing discussion that *mobility in public* is one of my key concerns.

UNITED STATES BLACK MODERNISM: *a black public-sphere mobility and fullness of United States black citizenship rights of locomotion, promotion, suffrage, occupational choice and compensation that yield what can only be designated a black-majority, politically participatory, bodily secure* GOOD LIFE.

The windows of opportunity for such United States black modernism have been few. Moreover, they have been of uncannily brief duration. Perhaps, the clearest, most unequivocal opening upon such black, mobile citizenship was the era of civil rights and black power during the 1950s, 1960s, and early 1970s. I believe the reason there have been only few and brief windows of black modernism is denoted and connoted in the United States by the single word *plantation*.

From the *Oxford English Dictionary* I sample these meanings of "plantation": "transplanting"; "laying out of wealth"; "settlement of persons in some locality, especially the planting of a colony"; "colonization"; "to send prisoners, etc. to the plantations, i.e. to penal service or indentured labour in the colonies"; "method of treating criminals of all kinds much in favour during the 17th century"; "plantation-Negro"; "plantation-slave."

The sign "plantation" moves in its connotations and denotations from active verb to nominal resultant. Transplantation of peoples from one locale to another, or establishment of a colony in "conquered" territory, results always in *penal* service and *plantation slavery.* We, therefore, turn South again in revisionary scholarship on black modernism in order to capture motion of signs such as *plantation, signs* that offer a genealogy of what must be designated black or African *immobilization*.

Nowadays it is fashionable in some scholarly circles to speak of "global modernity," engulfing with the phrase—in one colossal Atlantic embrace—thousands of particularities, geographical and demographic specificities of space, time, and place . . . as though to posit a paradigm as "global" is immediately and realistically to guarantee its analytical efficacy for any given locale. I salute and laud efforts at analytical generality and comprehensiveness. They can be speculative breaks with ethnocentrism, particularism, provinciality. Paul Gilroy's *The Black Atlantic: Modernity and Double Consciousness* represents such an effort.[5]

But I must confess immediately I have not discovered in Gilroy's analyses the specificity of time, place, and detail one requires to read (and, perhaps, empower) black United States modernism. I do not, however, mean to suggest by this judgment that Gilroy's postulates are without interest. His hypothesis that a "counterculture of modernity [was] produced by black intellectuals" (5) and requires survey is engaging. And his book as a whole charts a course of critique—an oceanic via media, as it were, between political praxis and popular culture enthusiasm. There are scholarly possibilities in abundance when Gilroy signals for his readers' attention the dread racial terror implicit in Euromodernity's Enlightenment project. However, for me, *The Black Atlantic* remains surprisingly abstract and indeterminate with respect to the very "chronotrope" the book claims as its analytical "organizing symbol"—namely, "ships in motion across the spaces between Europe, America, Africa, and the Caribbean" (4). After early mention, *ships* virtually disappear from Gilroy's work. They disappear as chronotropes, material vessels "transplanting" black populations, dread transports of "conquered" peoples to penal colonies of the Americas. *Ships*—as disciplinary and carceral "holds" on the shackled black body—receive no extensive treatment in *The Black Atlantic.*

Gilroy's neglect of material ships and their movement is in some respects understandable. For he is in the final analysis, far less committed to careful, multilocational history leading to greater comprehension of *plantations* than to issuing a sprightly monograph in the service of black diasporic music criticism. *The Black Atlantic*'s raison d'être, I believe, is exploration of African and diasporic black bodies engaged in expressive rebuttals, or lyrical "counters," to Hegelian and other corollary white Euro-American minds' dismissals of *blackness*. A fine raison d'être, to be sure.

Yet it is a motive that takes little account of actual ships . . . and finally . . . little multivocalic or multilingual account of an actual Atlantic Ocean. Effectively, *The Black Atlantic* returns Gilroy to his youthful authorial days, halcyon years when his chief preoccupation was popular music criticism. His Atlantic study is speculatively interesting, but chiefly in its sometimes strained decoding of lyrical and melodic intricacies and intentions of an at times Britishly "provincial" repertoire of black popular song. The peculiar form of Gilroy's work—its privileging of "the Atlantic"—ultimately rings (at least for me) a surprisingly English "changing same" on the old popular imperialist anthem "Rule Britannia! Britannia rules the Waves." I turn away, then, from Gilroy because I want to bring together *ships and plantations, determinately fixing attention on the privileged, locative site of my entire discussion—namely, the "South."*

III

In *The Atlantic Slave Trade,* Herbert Klein notes that "at the height of the [transatlantic slave] trade in the 1780s . . . some 260 or so ships, almost all with different owners, were needed to move the 79,000 slaves per annum who were sent to America."[6] In the mainland colonies of British North America, the preeminent destination of such ships was the "South." Klein observes:

> Although slaves were imported into every continental colony, there were only two really major centers of slave labor. The first region was the tidewater zone of the Chesapeake Bay, which included the colonies of Virginia, Maryland, and parts of North Carolina; and a second region further south centered on South Carolina and Georgia. . . . The Chesapeake became the primary tobacco producer for the world, exporting some 38 million pounds by 1700 and effectively liquidating English West Indian production. It was also the most important slave zone in continental North America, holding some 145,000 slaves (or 60 percent of the total in the thirteen colonies by 1750). (43)

A European "consumer revolution" demanding rice, sugar, tobacco, dyewoods, indigo, and ultimately megatonnage of cotton created the *labor demand* of, and from, southern *plantations.* Very material (as opposed to "chronotropic") and commercial ships, fitted out tightly and exactingly by ships' carpenters for the "transplantation" of black African bodies, were multiply "floating holds" of incarceration bringing a black-South majority to the New World. "Middle passage" describes the deadly Atlantic crossing from Africa to the Americas.

During the ships' passage, shackled black bodies were subject to perhaps the *ur*-definition of "tight places." For ships' carpenters allotted five square feet per body to black captives; "decks" or shelves were built for them between the hold and the main deck. "Any lowering of the slave deck, or extending it towards the bow or stern of the ship, in order to allow more room for the slaves, had the effect of reducing the area in which food and water casks could be stored.

But, on some ships, a second tier of wood would be set up within the slave deck, so as to allow a second assembly of captives to be carried in two narrower compartments."[7]

In the ships' cavities, twelve feet deep, human black "cargo" endured suffocating, fetid, torturous transport. The slave narrator Gustavus Vassa describes conditions of "slave decks" as follows: "The closeness of the place, and the heat of the climate, added to the number in the ship, which was so crowded that each had scarcely room to turn himself, almost suffocated us. . . . This wretched situation was again aggravated by the galling of the chains, now become insupportable; and the filth of the [latrine] tubs, into which the children often fell, and were almost suffocated. The shrieks of the women, and the groans of the dying, rendered a scene of horror almost inconceivable" (Thomas, 414). Afro-American poet Robert Hayden's magnificent "Middle Passage" captures the zone of confinement depicted by Vassa as a "voyage through death / to life upon these shores."[8]

So . . . *ships* . . . at least those analytically serving purposes of my present discussion are, for me historically and materially "prison ships." They journey from African incarceration (shackling) and sale of black bodies, *by black Africans on coasts of Africa*; they voyage through carceral, charnel "holds" of the middle passage; they deliver human "cargo" into disciplinary, penal protocols of *plantations* "South."

Logan's previously referenced statistics suggest there were nearly four million enslaved black bodies in the South at the commencement of the Civil War. This was the black majority, immobilized by slave law, confined by patrollers, overseers, drivers, sheriffs, and militia to southern agrarian abjection. One false move or movement easily resulted in death.

Of course, slavery at the South was marked (as recent labors of historian John Hope Franklin reveal) by "rebellious" transit—"absenting of self" and "running away"—of as many as fifty thousand black slaves in any given year.[9] Yet Frederick Law Olmstead's engaging report of his own southern ethnographies titled *A Journey in the Slave States* reveals the general efficacy of such "intra-plantation-state" black rebellious mobilization. Sojourning for a brief spell with the overseer of a Mississippi plantation, Olmstead learns the following of black "runaways": "Two months was the longest time any of them ever kept out. They [plantation 'technicians'] had dogs trained on purpose to run after niggers, and never let out for any thing else."[10]

Once inside plantation protocols and economies, the black situation was one of disciplined immobility and servile labor, whether in heavily surveilled and administered plantation fields or in strictly governed plantation domestic "house" service.

IV

"Penal" plantation protocols were the *telos* of the black body's journey through Atlantic incarceration to "life upon these shores." *Peasantry* is a euphemism with respect to the black-South body confined to Yazoo Delta or black "country district" agrarian arrangements of white profits. *Prisoner* is a vastly more accurate lexical item for what the *OED* designates as "plantation-Negro." For accepted ordinances of slave law and southern "Providence" unequivocally defined the black-South body as "justifiably" subjugated. The black-South body, according to southern wisdom and biblical exegesis, had transgressed God's law in Ham's viewing of his father Noah's nakedness. That body's uncomely and servile "blackness" cast it into darkness, outside the boundaries of the reasonably "human." Western philosophy, science, and common sense colored bestiality, wildness, savagery, and unreason as *black*. In *Race: The History of an Idea in the West,* Ivan Hannaford writes:

> The idea of freedom and equality enshrined in the U.S. Constitution was theoretically in conflict with chattel slavery but did not present much of a "political" problem until the 1830s because the Constitution had not envisaged that the Negro should, or ever could, be part of the natural societies envisioned by Hobbes, Locke, and Montesquieu. . . . Until the 1830s the Negro in North America was considered to be a slave by right of conquest, by empirical observation of natural difference, and by biblical exegesis;

> he was not a man by virtue of his membership as a good citizen of an Aristotelian, Ciceronian, or Machiavellian *res-publica.*[11]

"By right of conquest" translates, of course, as both *slave* and *prisoner.*

For the Harvard University Ph.D., W. E. B. Du Bois, as well as other Afro-American intellectuals of talented-tenth status such as the Reverend Alexander Crummell, the history of the transported African in the Americas may well have been the history of "double consciousness." No one was more eloquent than such men or more influential than their elite Negro Academy, in expressing the identity conundrum of blacks in America as an agonizing somatic and cognitive dissonance between being "Negro" *and* "American." They monumentally philosophized the angst of dual identity.

But for the black majority of the United States, "history" as such scarcely read out as a question of American "belonging." Certainly, the black-South majority of ships and plantations was propagandized, nearly to abject insanity, with the surety that their bodies *belonged,* unequivocally, to the white American planter class. American "history" thus reads out, in black-majority vocabularies, as *enslavement, incarceration, imprisonment.* The identity dilemma for the black majority is not captured by the declarative "One ever feels his two-ness," but rather by the interrogative *How do I break these all-too-real physical chains binding me?* The Afro-American jazz singer Nina Simone expresses the psychic import of this founding black-majority inquiry in the title of one of her most famous songs: "I wish I knew how it feels to be free!" Which might well translate as a black-majority urge for mobilization . . . beyond carceral *plantation* boundaries, transcending thick statistical protocols that have perennially sanctioned shackling the black body, its *lockdown in America.*

V

My claim is that turning south again facilitates our engagement with inescapable revisionary scholarly labors—work devoted to black-majority concerns and prompted, especially, by contemporary realities of a United States prison-industrial complex. "Turning

South again" yields—as I hope my foregoing discussion makes clear—a foreshadowing of high walls and "supermaximum security units" that seem less anomalous with respect to the black American majority experience with each clarion call (such as the brilliant Broadway production *Bring in 'Da Noise, Bring in 'Da Funk*'s masterful opening sequence danced by Savion Glover) of slave ships' litany of ironic names: "*Jesus, Estrella, Esperanza, Mercy* / Sails flashing to the wind like weapons."[12] Almost any given Afro-American historical configuration of people and events defined as "modernism" is, I believe, almost immediately historically discredited by continuous, fully documentable white American protocols of enslavement, criminalization, and punishment—the unceasing derogation of the black-South body.

It is, indeed, indisputable that "freedom" was the watchword of the incendiary Civil War. Casualties of that conflict outnumbered those of all other American wars combined. And in the estimate of historian Barbara Fields, the war only assumes a vestige of "humanity" if we interpret it as a conflict meant to "free" America's millions of black slaves. Yet we have already noted Cash's observation about the South's dedication—in complete collaboration with enormous financial, ideological, and political supports from other regions and governments of the United States—to immediate restoration, after the war, of "slavery" for the black majority. C. Vann Woodward asserts: "Apart from South Carolina, Louisiana, and Florida, where the Radicals [of Reconstruction managed] to prolong a troubled and contested authority for nearly [a decade], the Radical regime in the average state—from the time it was recognized by Congress till it was overthrown—lasted less than three and a half years" (22). Three and a half years is a desperately short space for a black majority in the millions—provisioned as Logan's citation above indicates, with virtually no capital or advanced skills—to "feel free." Three and a half years is less a window than a pinhole of light.

Moreover, even during the brief space of southern "Radicalism" in support of the thirteenth (abolition of slavery), fourteenth (equal protection), and fifteenth (suffrage) Civil War amendments to the Constitution, dramatic measures such as Mississippi's Black Codes were enacted literally to criminalize and reenslave the black majority. Vagrancy and enticement regulations and laws soon characterized the whole of the former Confederacy, with the "border state" of Kentucky signing on with alacrity. The actual "reconquest," as it were, of the "freed" black majority took form as thousands of arrests and imprisonments of blacks as the South experienced the birth, and extraordinarily rapid deployment against the black-South body, of a southern system of convict "lease labor."

If there needs to be a carceral "middle passage" (as historical "evidence" of the continuity of American protocols of black imprisonment) between enslavement, putative black "freedom," and today's United States private prison-industrial complex, that "passage" is marked out by southern convict lease labor.

As newly drafted "Negro Laws" mounted in number, southern jails and prisons were strained to their limits. Black "convictions" for such petty larceny as "theft" of a three-dollar suit could bring fines and court costs ranging up to a hundred dollars. Sentences in such cases could run in excess of ten years. Convicted blacks were seldom (if ever) equipped to pay exorbitant fines levied against them. Hence, they were released into the custody of the white person who covered their court costs and fines. Then the true incarceration began.

Terms of "working off" the debt incurred to one's white debtor might include hard labor in mining, turpentine manufacturing, or railroad-construction camps and, of course, on southern *plantations.* In the South, whole southern state systems of "criminal justice" became sinister arrangements for white criminalization of black bodies in order to supply labor demands of a New South.

In *"Worse Than Slavery": Parchman Farm and the Ordeal of Jim Crow Justice,* David M. Oshinsky offers the following account of convict leasing in Mississippi: "In 1868, [the businessman Edmund Richardson] struck a bargain with the federal authorities in Mississippi. . . . [He] needed cheap labor to work some land he had bought in the sparsely settled Yazoo Delta; the state had a gutted penitentiary overflowing with ex-slaves. The result was a contract that allowed Richardson to work these felons outside the prison walls. He promised to feed them, clothe them, guard them, and treat them well. The state agreed to pay him $18,000 a year for their maintenance and an additional sum for their transportation to and from his primitive Delta camps."[13] Convict leasing was a blatant, and strictly "for profit," shackling of the black-South body. And black convict labor came virtually to shape every industrial and agrarian "business" of the New South.

If documented and material ships transported black bodies through the "middle passage" of the Atlantic, then, eventually, such bodies in great mass were shunted about the South like beasts of labor: "On many railroads, convicts were moved from job to job in a rolling iron cage, which also provided their lodging at the site. The cage—eight feet wide, fifteen feet long, and eight feet high—housed upwards of twenty men. It was similar 'to those used for circus animals,' wrote a prison official, except it 'did not have the privacy which would be given to a respectable lion, tiger, or bear.'" (Oshinsky, 57)

Blackness—in a New South enamored of the abundant labor supply and profits to be reaped from black mass arrests—became synonymous with *crime*. Edward Ayers rightly notes that such a state of affairs "bred inhumane travesties": "In some of the most forbidding landscapes of the New South terrible scenes of inhumanity were played out: mass sickness, brutal whippings, discarded bodies, near starvation, rape."[14] Black convicts were forced at gunpoint and the lash's end to do the filthiest, most brutalizing, and dangerous labor required to build up and extract profit from "business" landscapes of the New South. Leased convicts slept on bare ground, were beaten without provocation, found themselves diseased without treatment, frostbitten, wounded from gunshot, suffering "shackle poisoning" (the constant rubbing of chains and leg irons against bare flesh). The most elaborated and enduring evolution of the southern convict lease system was represented by Mississippi's legendary Parchman Farm.

From *plantation* to "prison farm" is scarcely a liberating mobility toward *modernism*. Of Parchman Farm's financial returns for 1917, Oshinsky writes, "the penitentiary made a handsome profit in 1917. Unlike other prison systems, which drained public coffers at an ever-expanding rate, this one poured almost a million dollars into the state treasury through the sale of cotton and cotton seed. The figure was so astounding—it totaled almost half of Mississippi's entire budget for public education in 1917—that politicians and editors were soon calling Parchman the 'best prison' in America' " (155). Parchman was not condemned and closed until the 1970s!

VI

The foregoing discussion/projection of a carceral network that has continuously held the black-South body in a state of "suspended rights" may, indeed, render the introduction of Michel Foucault's formulations on *discipline* and *punishment* almost a discordant "theoretical" excess. However, I think it is impossible fully to comprehend the entailments of the black body's shackled passage from Elmina (slave baracoon on the African coast) to vermin-infested black-South conviction and sentencing at Parchman Farm—or to present-day, lockdown, death-row immobility in Hunstsville, Texas—*without* sampling the wisdom of Foucault. Foucault's brilliant genealogy of penality titled *Surveiller et punir* (in English translation, *Discipline and Punish*)[15] posits three stages of state response, or state apparatuses of "punishment," in the evolution of the prison.

Responses to "criminality" commence, according to Foucault, with public executions designed to display, for an eagerly assembled public, the power of the sovereign. This apparatus of public execution gives way to the chain gang and "cell cart" of mobile criminal "transport," resulting in what Foucault calls an "economy of suspended rights": "If it is still necessary for the law to reach and manipulate the convict, it will be at a distance, in the proper way, according to strict rules, and with a much 'higher aim' " (11).

In the second (chain gang) stage of State Response, the body itself is "criminalized" and "offense" enters what Foucault calls the "field of objects for study and judgment." (P. 11) "Technicians" of criminal justice, administrators of the law enter the picture; their "knowledge" becomes a way of "supervising" the individual as one object in a vast field of "attenuating circumstances" (18). Once "knowledge" enters Foucault's own field of exposition, conjunctions of punishment, technology, and "power" are predictable. It comes as no surprise when Foucault posits that a "technology of power" is the "very principle both of the humanization of the penal system and of the knowledge of man" (23).

In all-too-cryptic summation, let me say that for Foucault, the birth of the prison and the birth of the "human sciences" (i.e. "knowledge") are coterminous. The carceral economy—and a state "technology of power"—create "objects" in a field of study. The "knowledge" of *criminality* is silent; it constitutes a field where, ultimately, the "law" is reticent. Which is to say: once "death row" becomes the penal reality of day-to-day life, there is a manifest *disconnect* between the network constituted by *crime-trial-verdict-judge-sentencing-imprisonment* and the human sentience and actuality of the to-be-executed convict as *object*. A process of putative justice and its apparatus are silently (and now privately and for profit) folded into a field not only of "objects," but of objects destined for extermination.

Does this make sense?

What I want to say is that the silent "independence" of a privatized, corporate gulag of United States incarceration in the new century awaits—indeed summons—the extermination of Mumia Abu Jamal.

However, in our day-to-day United States life, we scarcely ever reflect that Texas, Louisiana, and Oklahoma—all southern territories of the actual present—are sites of mass black- and brown-body incarceration . . . and extermination. Huntsville, Texas, literally thrives on the death industry of a "silent" order long removed from the "law." It is the penal extermination capital of the USA. The "man of suspended rights" in our era, through the offices of *Wackenhut* and *Corrections Corporation of America* is "rentable property," chain gang occupant in Arizona, forced laborer, prison farm "felon" in North Carolina, cut down by guards' guns in his attempt to "escape" . . . silenced "occupant" of death row, like Mumia Abu Jamal.

From what sites do "models" for prisons derive?

Foucault suggests the following: factories (with their worklike regimen), monasteries (in their isolation), hospitals (which emphasize "cases" and "observation"), schools (governed by time "tables"), the military (a place of drills, obedience, standardizing mechanizations of the body). For society and the state, prisons function as apparatuses of confinement, knowledge, and power. They produce bodies disciplined to docility, creating *man-the-laboring-machine,* and man as "isolated" object produced and studied by the human sciences.

From the carnival of public execution, then, Foucault's analysis of the birth of the prison leads to a fascinating definition of "discipline." Matters of occupancy and vacancy that I have touched upon in my foregoing discussion reign supreme for Foucault. What do I mean?

Missing in what Foucault designates as the "disciplinary" project is what might be called "articulate vigilance of the law." Enclosed upon itself, partitioned off by cells (or spoon-fashion five-foot-square spaces of black-bodily confinement in the holds of slave prison ships), classified interchangeably by "rank"—the site of *discipline,* according to Foucault, consists of "methods, which made possible the meticulous control of the operations of the body, which assured the constant subjection of its forces and imposed upon them a relation of docility-utility" (137). "Discipline" draws up tables, prescribes movements, imposes exercises, arranges tactics (167). "The perfect disciplinary apparatus would make it possible for a single gaze to see everything constantly" (173). "Order," "control," "knowledge" derive from the body "suspended," relegated to a "field of objects"—transported, warehoused, worked by *Corrections Corporation of America* as the millennium turns.[16]

VII

On, and out of, what I want to call a *field of abjection*—an immobilizing suspension of black-South body rights of the southern "country districts"—Mr. Washington constructed and maintained his Tuskegee *plantation.* I think only a misconceived "apologetics" can fail, for whatever peculiar reasons, to read out the infamous

Tuskegee study of untreated syphilis in the black male as anything other than a *direct*, disciplinary, power-and-knowledge corollary of disciplinary enclosures, exercises, and tactics of the Tuskegee *plantation.* At Tuskegee, the law's "reticence" complicitly joined the silence of "medicine."

Isolated and insulated—even from its adjacent town—the Tuskegee plantation suspends rights of the black-South body at will. Informed of a staggering 36 percent syphilis infection rate of the black majority of Macon County, Washington's presidential successor at Tuskegee Institute, Robert Russa Moton, quipped: "I am surprised it is not 50 percent!" Tuskegee plantation's assumptions—deriving from powers of disciplinarity over the black "country districts"—responds to statistical "knowledge" with scandalous derogation, accusations of black "disease rampant." And the institute—from the concurrence of President Robert Russa Moton to the United States Public Health Service's design for a study of untreated syphilis in black males to its participation in "roundups" of black males as "objects in a field of medical knowledge," complete with spinal taps and X rays overseen by Tuskegee's Andrews Hospital . . . the institute abetted, "disciplined," "ranked," exercised its plantation-derived *powers* of death in complicity with the Nazi-like syphilis "experiment."

We might derive from Foucault's observations a proper judgment of correlations between prisons (read: *plantations*) and experimental knowledge (read: *medicine*). Foucault postulates that the "gaze" of examination (read: Tuskegee's roundups, spinal taps, and autopsies of black-South bodies) supplies the normalizing judgment of disciplinary technique (184). *Discipline* is, ultimately, a possibly exterminating "technology of power" (194).

In *Up from Slavery,* Booker T. Washington speaks of "getting hold" of Negroes of the country districts in their everyday life. Given the combined disciplinary protocols of Tuskegee—whose economies came to be "occupied," through time, by both a segregated Veterans Administration Hospital and a segregated military training ground for black airmen—can there be any wonder that Booker T. Washington felt, at the instant of his famous Atlanta address, like a "man on his way to the gallows"? He was, himself, a master executioner in masquerade.

VIII

Only under the literally revolutionary operations of the civil rights and black power movements of the 1950s and 1960s did the black-South body overcome the immobilizing and "damaged modernity" projected by the *plantation* and the *carceral* black oratorical canniness of Booker T. Washington on a fall day in Atlanta in 1895. The ultimate, achieved instance of *discipline* is defined by Foucault as the "panopticon." The panopticon is an enclosed and segmented space, observed at every point. Individuals incarcerated in the panopticon are inserted in a fixed place where their slightest movements are supervised and all events recorded. An uninterrupted work of panoptic writing links center and periphery, enabling power to be exercised without division and according to a continuous hierarchical arrangement. Shackled in the panopticon, individuals are constantly located, examined, distributed among living beings, the sick and the dead (197).

Here—under terms of the panopticon—is penal "immobilization" and access of medical "science" to the black-South body. Tuskegee implicitly promises such motionlessness and access to the state. In his engaging study *Black Leadership,* Manning Marable writes: "Every aspect of [the black students' movements at Tuskegee] fell under Washington's constant scrutiny. At mandatory religious exercises, all students had to pass by him for inspection. . . . Every day, Washington received extensive faculty reports on the smallest aspects of campus life: the 'daily poultry report,' the 'daily swine herd report,' the state of the latrines, the 'condition of the kitchens.' "[17]

If chain gang display constitutes a "theater of punishment," then Washington's immobilizing scrupulosity of the visual comprises a "minipanopticon unto itself." It is a southern disciplinary plantation regulation of "Negro affairs"; it is indisputably implicated in a disciplinary "South" conceived as an emblem of America writ locally.

It is surely to the South—as emblem or metonym for American "disciplinarity"—that I feel we must turn again. The "South," for

America's cultural studies scholars, must be in us. Acknowledging its ambivalent irony, I would like to conclude with lines from a famous Parchman Farm prison song: "It ain't but one thing I done wrong / I stayed in Mississippi just a day too long." The United States at large is always already in Mississippi, and Mississippi—for better or worse for black modernism—is always in the United States.

Fortunately, though, black-South blues traditions are as improvisatory and situational as they are southern. In the present instant, they empower us to alter the sign "Mississippi" to read "Alabama." Staying in "Alabama" for days too long carries us beyond Tuskegee zones of discipline and confinement and through time to the righteous civil rights motions of the black-South body. We find ourselves in the extraordinary company of Mrs. Rosa Parks and the Reverend Dr. Martin Luther King . . . just one hour down the road from Mr. Washington's *plantation.* Black modernism in historical progress has bright birth in Montgomery. Breaking the frame. In 2000, such modernism waits to be academically and politically shaped into a black-South, black-majority public-sphere mobility for a new century.

Notes

Prologue

1 Etheridge Knight, *Born of a Woman: New and Selected Poems* (Boston: Houghton Mifflin, 1980), pp. 26–27.
2 Alan Hyde, *Bodies of Law* (Princeton, N.J.: Princeton University Press, 1997), p. 231.
3 Robert Hayden, *Angle of Ascent: New and Selected Poems* (New York: Liveright, 1975), pp. 118–123.
4 David M. Oshinsky, *"Worse Than Slavery": Parchman Farm and the Ordeal of Jim Crow Justice* (New York: Free Press, 1996), p. 145.
5 Roger Jaco, "Killing Time," in *Doing Time: 25 Years of Prison Writing*, ed. Bell Gale Chevigny (New York: Arcade, 1999).

Modernism's Performative Masquerade

1 Ralph Ellison, *Invisible Man* (New York: Random House, 1953). All citations refer to this edition and are hereafter noted in the text by page numbers in parentheses.
2 Booker T. Washington, *Up from Slavery,* quoted in John Hope Franklin, *Three Negro Classics,* (New York: Avon, 1995). All citations refer to this edition and are hereafter noted in the text by page numbers in parentheses.
3 William Faulkner, *Absalom, Absalom* (New York: Vintage International, 1986), p. 303. All citations hereafter refer to this edition.
4 W. J. Cash, *The Mind of the South* (New York: Knopf, 1941), p. 107.
5 James C. Cobb, *Redefining Southern Culture: Mind and Identity in the Modern South* (Athens: University of Georgia Press, 1999), p. 61.
6 Ibid., p. 73. Zinn's words are drawn from Cobb's discussion.

7 Ibid., p. 58.

8 Quoted in *The Federalist,* ed. Jacob Cooke (New York: Meridian, 1961), p. 63. My emphasis.

9 Patricia Yaeger, "Consuming Trauma; or, The Pleasure of Merely Circulating," *Journal X,* 1 (spring 1997), pp. 225–251. All citations are hereafter noted in the text by page numbers in parentheses.

10 Orlando Patterson, *Slavery and Social Death: A Comparative Study* (Cambridge, Mass.: Harvard University Press, 1987).

11 Erving Goffman, *Frame Analysis: An Essay on the Organization of Experience* (Cambridge, Mass.: Harvard University Press, 1974). All citations are noted in the text by page numbers in parentheses.

12 Victor Turner, *The Forest of Symbols: Aspects of Ndembu Ritual* (Ithaca, N.Y.: Cornell University Press, 1967), pp. 93–97.

13 For more on black (w)holeness and the scene of black South performance see my book *Blues, Ideology and Afro-American Literature* (Chicago: University of Chicago Press, 1984), pp. 154–155.

14 See Henry Louis Gates Jr., *The Signifying Monkey: A Theory of African-American Literary Criticism* (New York: Oxford University Press), 1988, pp. 44–54.

15 Paul Laurence Dunbar, "We Wear the Mask," in *The Norton Anthology of African American Literature,* ed. Henry Louis Gates Jr. and Nellie McKay (New York: W. W. Norton, 1997), p. 896.

16 Erving Goffman, *The Presentation of Self in Everyday Life* (Garden City, N.Y.: Doubleday, 1959), p. 72.

17 *Diagnostic and Statistical Manual of Mental Disorders,* 4th ed. (Washington: American Psychiatric Association, 1995).

18 Arnold Rampersad, "Psychology and Afro-American Biography," *Yale Review,* 1 (1989): 6.

19 W. E. B. Du Bois, *The Souls of Black Folk* (New York: Penguin, 1982), p. 50. All citations hereafter refer to this edition. On the implications of the doctrine of *partus sequitur ventrem* see Hortense Spiller's "Mama's Baby Papa's Maybe: An American Grammar Book," *Diacritics* 17 (summer 1987): 67.

20 Erving Goffman, *Asylums: Essays on the Social Situation of Mental Patients and Other Inmates* (Chicago: Aldine, 1961), pp. 1–125.

21 Leon Higgonbotham, *In the Matter of Color, Race and the American Legal Process: The Colonial Period* (New York: Oxford University Press, 1972), p. 38. All citations are hereafter noted in the text by page numbers in parentheses.

22 James Baldwin, *Notes of a Native Son* (New York: Dial, 1963), p. 29.

23 Louis R. Harlan, *Booker T. Washington: The Making of a Black Leader, 1856–1901* (New York: Oxford University Press, 1972). All citations are hereafter noted in the text by page numbers in parentheses.
24 Mary Douglas, *Purity and Danger* (New York: Routledge, 1966), p. 35.
25 Carlyle speaks of the heroic "Great Man" in these encomiastic terms: "For, as I take it, Universal History, the history of what man has accomplished in this world, is at bottom the History of the Great Men who have worked. They were the leaders of men, these great ones; the modellers . . . and in a wide sense creators, of whatsoever the general mass of men contrived to do or attain; all things that we see standing accomplished in the world are properly the outer material result, the practical realisation and embodiment, of Thoughts that dwell in the Great Men sent into the world: the soul of the whole world's history, it may justly be considered, were the history of these." *On Heroes and Hero Worship and the Heroic in History* (Lincoln: University of Nebraska Press, 1966), p. 1.
26 Jacques Lacan, *Écrits: A Selection,* trans. Alan Sheridan (New York: Norton, 1977), pp. 281–291.
27 Richard Wright, "Between the World and Me," in *Richard Wright Reader,* ed. Ellen Wright and Michel Fabre (New York: Harper and Row, 1978), pp. 246–247.
28 Walter White, *Rope and Faggot* (New York: Arno, 1969). The novel first appeared in the 1920s.
29 Lillian Smith, *Strange Fruit* (Athens: University of Georgia Press, 1985). The novel first appeared in 1944. In ruminating upon lynching Billie Holiday lyrically intones, "[B]lack bodies swayin' in the southern breeze."
30 The black James Byrd Jr. was walking along a Texas road when offered a ride by white men in a pickup truck. The group of whites included ex-convict members of the white supremacist organization the Aryan Brotherhood. They roped Byrd to the back of the pickup and dragged him to horrendous death.
31 Walter Benjamin, *Charles Baudelaire: A Lyric Poet in the Era of High Capitalism,* trans. Harry Zohn (London: NLB, 1973). All citations are hereafter noted in the text by page numbers in parentheses.
32 Sander Gilman, *Freud, Race, and Gender* (Princeton, N.J.: Princeton University Press, 1993).
33 Lacan, *Écrits,* p. 316.
34 See Eric Lott, *Love and Theft: Blackface Minstrelsy and the American Working Class* (New York: Oxford University Press, 1993), and David

Roediger, *The Wages of Whiteness: Race and the Making of the American Working Class* (New York: Verso, 1991).

35 As Alan Sheridan (*Écrits,* translator's note, p. ix) suggests, the symbolic order acts as a frame that shapes the human subject. Sheridan defines the Lacanian symbolic order as a "relationship" between the human subject and "signifiers, speech [and] language." "The symbolic" is distinguished from "the imaginary," which for Lacan is a realm derived from the relationship "between the ego and its images." Thus frame (or stage) precedes (racialized) identity in America.

36 The entry into "language" is the occupancy of the "symbolic order." This order is the "limit" of the social and the frame for rational subjectivity.

37 Joan Riviere, "Womanliness as Masquerade," reprinted in *Formations of Fantasy,* ed. Victor Burgin, James Donald, and Cora Kaplan (New York: Routledge, 1989), pp. 35–44.

38 Stephen Heath, "Joan Riviere and the Masquerade," in Burgin et al., *Formations of Fantasy,* pp. 45–61.

39 Frederick Douglass, *Narrative of the Life of Frederick Douglass,* ed. Houston A. Baker (New York: Penguin, 1982), p. 112; William Faulkner, *Absalom, Absalom* (New York: Random House, 1936), pp. 28–30.

40 Rhonda Gaerlick, *Rising Star: Dandyism, Gender, and Performance in the Fin de Siècle.* (Princeton, N.J.: Princeton University Press, 1998).

41 Louis Harlan, *Booker T. Washington: The Wizard of Tuskegee, 1910–1915* (New York: Oxford University Press, 1983), pp. 451–452.

42 The fullest account of the "experiment" or "study" is found in James Jones's *Bad Blood: The Tuskegee Syphilis Experiment* (New York: Free Press, 1993). I have relied heavily upon Jones's work in my characterization of "what happened" at Tuskegee and because of Tuskegee's compliance.

A Concluding Meditation on Plantations, Ships, and Black Modernism

1 Rayford Logan, *The Betrayal of the Negro: From Rutherford B. Hayes to Woodrow Wilson* (New York: Da Capo, 1997), p. 117. All citations refer to this edition and are hereafter noted in the text by page numbers in parentheses. Logan's work first appeared in 1954 under the title *The Negro in American Life and Thought: The Nadir, 1877–1901.* The fine Da Capo edition contains an illuminating introduction by Eric Foner.

2 C. Vann Woodward, *Origins of the New South, 1877–1913* (Baton Rouge:

Louisiana State University Press, 1997), p. 367. All citations refer to this edition and are hereafter noted in the text by page numbers in parentheses.

3 Robert J. Norrell, *Reaping the Whirlwind; The Civil Rights Movement in Tuskegee* (New York: Knopf, 1998), pp. 26–27. All citations refer to this edition and are hereafter noted in the text by page numbers in parentheses.

4 Houston A. Baker Jr., "Critical Memory and the Black Public Sphere" in *The Black Public Sphere,* ed. Black Public Sphere Collective (Chicago: University of Chicago Press, 1995), pp. 5–37.

5 Paul Gilroy, *The Black Atlantic: Modernity and Double Consciousness* (Cambridge; Harvard University Press, 1993). All citations are hereafter noted in the text by page numbers in parentheses.

6 Herbert S. Klein, *The Atlantic Slave Trade.* (Cambridge: Cambridge University Press, 1999), p. 99. All citations are hereafter noted in the text by page numbers in parentheses.

7 Hugh Thomas, *The Slave Trade: The Story of the Atlantic Slave Trade, 1492–1870.* (New York: Capricorn, 1959), p. 4. All citations refer to this edition and are hereafter noted in the text by page numbers in parentheses.

8 Robert Hayden, "Middle Passage," in *The Norton Anthology of African American Literature,* ed. Henry Louis Gates Jr. and Nellie McKay (New York: W. W. Norton, 1997), p. 1501.

9 John Hope Franklin and Loren Schweninger, *Runaway Slaves: Rebels on the Plantation.* (New York: Oxford University Press, 1999).

10 Frederick Law Olmstead, *The Slave States,* ed. Harvey Wish (New York: Capricorn, 1959), p. 202.

11 Ivan Hannaford, *Race: The History of an Idea in the West* (Baltimore, Md.: Johns Hopkins University Press, 1996), p. 270.

12 Robert Hayden, "Middle Passage," *Angle of Ascent: New and Selected Poems* (New York: Liveright, 1975), pp. 118–123.

13 David M. Oshinsky, *"Worse than Slavery": Parchman Farm and the Ordeal of Jim Crow Justice* (New York: Free Press, 1996), p. 35. All citations are hereafter noted by page numbers in parentheses.

14 Edward L. Ayers, *The Promise of the New South: Life after Reconstruction* (New York: Oxford University, 1992), p. 154.

15 Michel Foucault, *Discipline and Punish* (New York: Penguin, 1979). All citations refer to this edition and are hereafter noted in the text by page numbers in parentheses.

16 An article detailing the workings of the private prison-industrial com-

plex appeared in the December 1998 issue of the *Atlantic,* vol. 282. (Boston: The Atlantic Monthly Co.), 58–77.

17 Manning Marable, *Black Leadership* (New York: Columbia University Press, 1998), p. 28.

Index

Houston A. Baker Jr. is the Susan Fox and George D. Beischer Arts and Sciences Professor of English and Professor of African and African American Studies at Duke University. He is the editor of the journal *American Literature* and the author of numerous books of literary criticism and poetry.

Library of Congress Cataloging-in-Publication Data
Baker, Houston A.
Turning south again : re-thinking modernism/re-reading Booker T. / by Houston A. Baker Jr.
p. cm.
Includes bibliographical references (p.) and index.
ISBN 0-8223-2686-8 (cloth: alk. paper)
ISBN 0-8223-2695-7 (pbk. : alk. paper)
1. Afro-Americans—Southern States—Social conditions. 2. Afro-Americans—Civil rights—Southern States—History. 3. Southern States—Race relations. 4. Washington, Booker T., 1856–1915—Political and social views. 5. Washington, Booker T., 1856–1915—Criticism and interpretation. 6. Tuskegee Institute. 7. Modernism (Literature)—Southern States—History. 8. Afro-Americans—Southern States—Intellectual life. I. Title.
E185.92 .B35 2001
305.896′073075—dc21 00-011129